D0078691

Suicide Prevention

Recent Titles in Psychology Briefs

SUICIDE
PREVENTION

❖

Kristine Bertini

Psychology Briefs

PRAEGER™

An Imprint of ABC-CLIO, LLC
Santa Barbara, California • Denver, Colorado

Library of Congress Cataloging-in-Publication Data

Bertini, Kristine, 1955-
  Suicide prevention / Kristine Bertini.
    pages cm.—(Psychology briefs)
  Includes bibliographical references and index.
  ISBN 978-1-4408-4191-0 (hardback)—ISBN 978-1-4408-4192-7 (ebook)
1. Suicide—Prevention. I. Title.
  RC569.B47 2016
  616.85′8445—dc23   2015036586

ISBN: 978-1-4408-4191-0
EISBN: 978-1-4408-4192-7

20 19 18 17 16   1 2 3 4 5

This book is also available on the World Wide Web as an eBook.
Visit www.abc-clio.com for details.

Praeger
An Imprint of ABC-CLIO, LLC

ABC-CLIO, LLC
130 Cremona Drive, P.O. Box 1911
Santa Barbara, California 93116-1911

This book is printed on acid-free paper ∞
Manufactured in the United States of America

For my father and hero, George Eugene Bertini

Contents

Introduction:
Understanding Suicide

The potato is a hearty vegetable. Many farmers leave their potatoes in dark burlap sacks in root cellars while they harvest. When a pinpoint of light emerges through a broken or dirty window in the cellar, the potato will seek this brightness with all its might. The potato's eye will find the light filtered by the sun and attempt to grow upwards towards life.

In an inner city with sidewalks that are crusted over by layers of pavement and cement, a sprout of grass will find its way up through a dry crack in the ground. This lone blade of grass will go unnoticed by the daily crowds of people who tramp over it. Yet it reaches up, like a small flag to the heavens, only to be trodden upon again and again. It is determined to have its moment in the light.

In small, dank ponds across the planet tiny amoebic creatures survive by feeding off the decaying substances that fall to the bottom of the pond. Without conscious thought these creatures automatically seek survival. When the rains dwindle and the pond evaporates, these tiny, nearly invisible creatures seek other moisture to maintain their existence.

Life, even at the most primitive level, seeks to replenish itself and survive. In some of the most devastating circumstances and horrific conditions, the human spirit fights to stay alive. Stories of individuals who have survived concentration camps, war crimes, family abuse, and near fatal accidents give us evidence of just how strong the human spirit can be under the most catastrophic of circumstances.

This instinctual fight for life that permeates most people's existence can make it very difficult to understand why some individuals want to die and, in fact, take their own lives by suicide. Unfortunately, suicide is not an uncommon phenomenon. In the United States a suicide attempt is made every 18 minutes, and suicide claims the lives of more than 40,000 people each year.

This book provides a basic understanding of suicide and of recovery for the suicidal person. To create better insight into the suicidal mind, we look at the factors that can lead to self-destructive acts. Some of the very first seeds for suicidal thoughts may be planted as the fetus develops in the womb. These early seeds of suicidal predisposition may provide clues to why people kill themselves.

The investigation into the suicidal mind is not a simple one. The path to completed suicide is complex and generally has multiple causes, which culminate in one final act of desperation. Each person who completes suicide has his or her own unique trajectory that leads down a path to self-inflicted death.

Yes, seeds for an individual's suicidal predisposition may be planted very early in the infant's development, but there are also factors that can act as interventions to the development of suicidal intent. While this book will examine specific vulnerabilities to suicide and why some individuals may be predisposed to suicidal intent, it will more importantly focus on the resiliencies that can be fortified or built within the suicidal person. These important human strengths are identified and emphasized in models for recovery for the suicidal individual. Resiliency is a key factor in suicide intervention, and a basic recovery program for the suicidal person includes personalized coping and resiliency-building skills. A clear and specific model of recovery for the suicidal individual is included in this book, which specifies methods for accessing help and a plan for positive action. Once a recovery plan can be put in place, imminent self-harm is reduced as supports are increased. There is hope for the suicidal person; this hope needs to be highlighted and understood. A predisposition for suicide is not a fatal diagnosis for completed suicide.

In the tragic situation when an individual completes suicide, there are survivors who are left behind. Loved ones, friends, and colleagues are left to make sense of what may appear to be a meaningless act. Each of the completed suicides in the United States every year touches at least six other people in profound and life-altering ways, meaning some 240,000— nearly a quarter of a million—surrounding people are affected and often traumatized. The impact of a loved one's suicide on family members, friends, co-workers, and acquaintances creates ripples of aftershocks that may run deeply and last for years in those who experience the loss. Those left behind grieve; they try to understand and make meaning of the suicide, but often there is no complete closure or satisfactory answer to the question of "Why?" While there may not be concrete, clear answers regarding why someone commits suicide, there are certainly clues that can help those left behind to find peace.

Beyond the information and strategies that are provided in *Suicide Prevention*, there is an underlying and at times direct theme throughout the book that explores how humankind makes meaning of life and death. This meaning comes from cultural factors, environment, genetics, experiences, and a variety of sources that combine to make each person unique.

The topic of suicide is profound and exposes some of the biggest questions and fears that we have regarding life and death. While the materials in this book reflect the serious nature of the subject, it is hoped that the theme of resiliency will shine through the pages and help the reader to find words of hope, comfort, and healing. The human spirit has the intrinsic ability and tools to seek life with greater resolve than a potato, a sprout of grass, or a tiny amoeba. The desire to live is instinctual, and when pain and suffering can be diminished, the life force fortifies, magnifies, and blossoms again.

This book provides a map of how the suicidal mind can develop. More importantly, however, a map of recovery is presented for anyone who may be thinking about taking his or her own life. When the force of life is beaten or worn down by internal or environmental factors, this book can become a resource to find new hope and a plan for replenishment of a battered soul. Stories in this book will provide insight into recovery and resiliency from individuals who were once suicidal and who have come back from the edge of death and are finding joy in their daily lives. There will be highlighted examples of how to identify and help the person who may be suicidal. Intervention by a concerned other can indeed be instrumental in stopping a death. And, as there will be some people who will still choose the path of suicide, the words in this book may also provide some solace for those left behind and help them to make meaning of their loss.

May we find comfort in each other.

1

❖❖❖

How Suicidal Thoughts Can Find Their Beginnings

The little one sleeps in its cradle, I lift the gauze and look a long time, and silently brush away flies With my hand . . .

Walt Whitman

CASE EXAMPLE: FRAGILE START

Three Scenarios of Early Beginning

An infant cries. The baby's inner city parent reaches into the bureau drawer and pulls the child out and close to the chest, the heart. Soothing, cooing love sounds from the adult radiate through the child. Gentle and tender touches and rocking motions lull the infant into an altered state of reverie. Love is transmitted from the parent to the child with every movement, touch, and sound. The infant gurgles and safely nestles into the crook of a sheltering arm.

Another infant cries. Its parent is distracted and impatient with the sound. Feeling disturbed and interrupted, this parent reaches for the infant. The parent's touch is not gentle. The infant arches its back and responds with louder cries. The adult bounces the infant in an up-and-down motion in the hope that the crying will stop, but the child wails all the more loudly. The parent feels frustration at the infant's continuous needs, and the bouncing becomes more pronounced. The infant unconsciously picks up the parent's resentment and reacts with its own rage until it cries itself into a fitful, sweating sleep.

A third infant awakes in its crib. Its cries are unheard. It is not picked up or held. It is wet and hungry. Its fists shake in rage and unknown terror. The parent is sleeping, or away, or in a drug-induced state. The infant wails, and in time hands reach into the crib and pick up the child. These hands are not the parent's hands. They belong to another adult and seek to quiet the sounds of the child. The parent responds only intermittently and with ambivalence, and the infant is left to the devices of the world.

These three scenarios illustrate how the first months in an infant's life can impact them through a sense of deep love, indifference, neglect, or abuse. Each infant internalizes these sensations as they grow in their new world.

In The Womb

In a mere instant in time, sperm melts into an egg, and a baby is conceived in a womb. The fates determine much of how and where this infant will begin its life and what the internal and external conditions that impact the womb will be as the fetus develops. The baby's parents may be wealthy or poor; they may reside in a Third World country or in an urban, metropolitan city. The child may be born in perfect health or with any number of medical issues. The infant's parents may have been awaiting the birth of their child with joy and excitement, or the parents may be despairing that their child is being brought into the world. According to Ellenor Mittendorfer-Rutz and others, good mothering begins well before the day of birth.

A pregnant woman may shelter the child growing in her womb from the world's harshness by limiting her contact with loud sounds, violent people, and images that disturb her own emotions. This mother may be a woman of privilege who has the financial, physical, and emotional resources to surround herself with loving others, good nutrition, and calming music. The fetus is honored and cherished, and the mother cares for her body, so the child will grow in a womb protected from negative outside forces. As this mother limits her own stress, her fetus grows in an environment that is stable and unmarked by trauma. This fetus unconsciously begins to sense the world as a loving and consistent place.

In contrast, another mother may live in a world that is laced with turmoil. There may be violent others in this woman's environment who impact her emotional health and feelings of well-being. The fetus can feel the vibrations of this mother's stress, and negative electrical charges will penetrate the tiny cells that are forming. Some mothers may not have the resources to provide proper nutrition for the growing fetus, and this can also impact the development of the growing child. Drinking alcohol, smoking cigarettes, and using substances can also affect the fetus. Other influences, such as the parents' biology and heredity, may affect the growing fetus. Medical issues that can impact later functioning in the world may begin in the early formation of the cells as they are transmitted from one generation to another, from parent to forming child. The groundwork for genetically transmitted physical imperfections such as multiple sclerosis, cancer, and Alzheimer's is laid in the first months of life. Other biologically carried seeds from the parents may be planted for later mental health issues such as depression, attention deficit disorder, and anxiety.

Environmental and biological parenting factors in the early development of the fetus may seem formidable and can be the precursor for later issues in life. They are important to note, as they, indeed, play a role in the character of the infant. However, in Chapter 3 the individual's resiliencies and vulnerabilities are detailed, and these qualities can be seen to alter the course of biology and the environment in an individual's life. Fate has its moment in the creation of the fetus and child; self-determination of the individual will also be seen to have its place.

Attachment

The early attachment of the infant to its caregivers can create the foundation for all relationships to come in the child's life. Donald Winnicott described the infant's environment as being a critical factor in the healthy development of the child. He believed that when the environment is good enough, it can foster the maturational processes of the infant. Winnicott used the term "good enough mother" to describe the parental role of providing sufficiently for the child to get a good start in life. He believed that when the parent is successful at meeting the infant's gestures and needs, the child's development will include genuine, happy, and spontaneous behaviors. Winnicott also believed that if the environment is not safe, the individual builds up a false set of relationships. Indeed, most theorists conclude that early attachment patterns of the infant and child influence later relationship patterns.

It is satisfying to think about the child that is born into a family of good emotional resources. The caregivers are able to provide the child with emotional comfort that is necessary to design a healthy internal world; this child is held and supported through all the travails that he will face and learns just how to navigate the planet under the watchful eye of his parent. This youngster will be taught the skills to master the emotional challenges that life throws at him. This child will grow into an adult who can adapt to change and to the inevitable hardships that are bound to confront him in life. Although this person may be surrounded by some early difficulties such as poverty or a biological illness, he will also have learned through good parenting that he can master and survive these difficulties.

The world has many barriers to developing a healthy sense of self. However, when an infant grows up in a home that is supportive and loving, a foundation is created in which the developing self will flourish, even under adversity. The toddler who is praised and rewarded for good behavior will begin to cement the knowledge within herself that she is lovable and worthy. Her self-esteem will be built first from the outside in; as she is provided with positive reinforcement, she will eventually come to believe that she is, indeed, a treasure to the world. This internalization of self-worth will fortify the child through challenging times, building further resiliency as she masters life's difficulties.

In comparison, the infant and developing child who does not have loving and consistent parenting faces the world at a great disadvantage. Sigmund Freud wrote that anxiety in children is nothing other than an expression of the fact that they are feeling the loss of affection from the person that they love. Imagine the child who is left to master his environment without consistent love and support. This child's basic needs of food and shelter may be satisfied, but her need for parental affection and consistent parenting is absent. In some cases, the child is not only reared in an environment of passive neglect, but emotional or physical abuse may also be present. This child may be subject to a resentful and angry parent, from which a foundation of fear and anxiety is created. The growing person may witness rage that is manifested in a loved one being battered by another, or the child may experience physical harm herself. How can this child develop a healthy sense of self? What does this child learn about the world and others in it?

The first task of the child that is raised in an unsafe environment is to survive. Children learn quickly that if a caregiver is violent, there can be ways to avoid harm. These methods of avoidance come at great cost to the developing self. Spontaneity and genuine wants and feelings must be pushed below the surface, and a pretend self may be created. This pretend self becomes a complex combination of accommodation and/or resistance to the adult's needs, and an underlying development of significant rage or depression can begin. As the child grows, its protective accommodation or resistance strategies become more sophisticated and the genuine self is more deeply buried. These accommodations are extremely functional during childhood as they serve to keep the child safe from the parent's wrath. However, as the child becomes an adult, the old defensive patterns are no longer functional and impact the sense of self, well-being, and relationships with others.

Compounding environmental stressors that affect a child's development will be any hereditary factors that have been transmitted from the parent or developed uniquely in the growing youngster. These factors could include physical impairments such as hearing loss, bone structure deficits, speech difficulties, or a variety of other issues. Medical challenges experienced by the child also can significantly impact the relationship between parent and child. The adult may come to find the many necessary hospital trips and doctor's appointments a frustration, and, thus, the child may come to feel like a burden to the family. If the parent is unable to provide the ill or disabled child with supportive care and understanding, this child can experience distress that results not only from the illness, but also from the lack of compassion from the loved one.

Children who inherit mental health issues from their parents, such as depression, anxiety, attention deficit disorder, bipolar disorder, autism, and, in later years, substance dependence also experience a disadvantage if they do not have a parent who is understanding and responsive to the specific nature of the illness. These issues may become exaggerated when the loved ones react with anger, distaste, or even hostility to behaviors that result from the child's mental illness. Instead of helping the child to learn to manage his symptoms and flourish, the parent who misunderstands mental health issues may instead further push the child into a deeper state of disruption.

The early caregiver's reactions to the physical and mental health issues of the child can create long-term responses from the child that can impact her feelings about self and others in later adulthood. The dynamics that are set in place in early infancy and childhood are powerful legacies that impact the adult profoundly.

Among the many factors that influence the development of the child are the cultural, religious, and social allegiances the family has formed. These factors may be multigenerational and contribute to the image the family has created for itself and instills into the new family member. For example, being born into a family that is part of an underrepresented ethnic group has its own unique compilation of responses that affect how the child may greet the world around him. If this family has been treated with bigotry and hatred, it is likely that the child will pick up wariness, anger, and mistrust from his parents. The sense of the child's self will be impacted by how the world has responded to his family's not being a part of the privileged majority. The same can be said for a child that is born to poverty, or to a religion that is not part of the mainstream culture. Difference can breed fear and prejudice, and cultural factors are sometimes the focus of hate crimes from others who are full of ignorance and rage. At very young ages children can instinctually understand when they are not revered. While a child may not understand the reasons for bigotry, it can be internalized and create significant issues with himself and others.

Some family cultural attributes may be more visible than those of other cultures. A child born into an African American family is black, and the color of her skin tells the world her ethnicity. An Iranian child also will look different from the mainstream white culture in the United States, and her difference could propel a bigoted person to act in hatred. A person of Russian descent, however, may appear to be from the mainstream white culture and therefore may not experience acts of discrimination.

On the other hand, if a child is born into a cultural group that is part of the privileged majority or mainstream culture, he may feel more accepted simply as a result of his culture. These children will not have to manage prejudice inflicted by fear of difference. They can more easily settle in to their homogenous communities and never even have to consider what it might be like to be a person of difference.

The cultural norms of the family can also have a significant impact on the child. Cultural norms are adopted by family systems and are often unspoken ways in which the family interacts and relates to the outside world. Some family norms are invisible, such as being born into a family that is stoic in nature and does not express feelings or ask for assistance from others in their community. Cultural values such as these can be transmitted nonverbally, and the child that is raised in a stoic environment may learn by witnessing others in the home that her family does not show vulnerability. This child may hold feelings in and isolate herself. The cultural norms of an African American family may also be invisible to the outside eye. While this family may face bigotry due to its African American culture and difference in appearance, which is visible, they may also have invisible differences, such as religious beliefs that are not the same as those of the mainstream norm. The child born into this family may experience both the multigenerational pain of African American oppression and the present moment impact of religious difference.

The child makes meaning in his world through his own experiences and by watching his caregivers interact with him and others in his environment. Each caregiver comes with his own history and culture, his own positive and negative dealings with the world. As the child witnesses the adult interact with others around him, the child begins to make his own meaning from these interactions. The growing person may begin to see the world as a good and safe place if that is what the parent believes and how the parent interacts. Or, if the parent is fearful of others, the child may begin to interpret the outside world as a dangerous place.

Carl Jung wrote about the collective unconscious and in his work described how images, thoughts, feelings, and behaviors can be transmitted for generations between groups, families, and individuals. According to Jung's theory of the collective unconscious, a child born into a family that has descended from tragedy many generations ago may pick up and carry the unresolved grief or rage from decades past. This child may not be aware of where or how the sadness originated, but it could be an underlying emotion to the formation of the self, transmitted through the generations. The impact of the collective unconscious is a fascinating twist to the child's development. Fate, environment, heredity, culture, and the past all combine to design a child's formation. In the remainder of this chapter the early development of suicidal tendencies will be tied to each of these factors.

The Seeds of Suicide

. . . And as to you Life I reckon you are the leavings of many deaths,
(no doubt I have died myself ten thousand times before).

                                                            Walt Whitman

It would seem to be simple common sense that a child who experiences a warm and loving childhood will grow into a secure and well-adapted adult. It is important to note that many children grow to be healthy and functional members of society. Even in the healthiest of homes, children may experience moments when their parents are not available or are distracted or even neglectful. However, in the homes that develop a positive sense of self in the child, the moments of caring and love far outnumber the moments of parenting failures. Every parent will have many moments of distraction and emotional unavailability to the child. When a parent has an illness or is facing a challenge at work or experiences a serious life event, it is obvious that this parent will not be entirely attentive to the child. However, the inattention will be short lived, and the overall attachment of parent to child will be positive and attuned.

Conversely, it is not rocket science to predict that a child raised in an environment lacking empathy and consistency may experience later life problems. The extent of these later life problems may be determined by the levels of ambivalence, antipathy, neglect, or abuse experienced by the child. Children are dependent on their parents from the moment they are born. They arrive into the world somewhat a blank slate, and they learn from their environment and the people who are closest to them. If they have caregivers who are not loving and consistent with them, they will have a core foundation that is not secure and is vulnerable to life's many challenges.

In a significant study by Barbara M. Richards, she concludes that in the view of psychotherapists over half the patients who have attempted or succeeded in completing suicide have experienced rejection and abandonment in their early years. Parents were often perceived as absent and unavailable, and a high percentage of the patients reported feeling disconnected from their mother and father. These individuals developed a bleak, impoverished inner world, which contributes to suicidal thoughts, feelings, and actions. In a home with unavailable, emotionally neglectful caregivers, the child is left to her own devices, and the internal development of the self is based on impressions the child can gather in this void. The lack of mirroring of the self leaves the child to design her own vision of who she is in the world. Because the craving for love and support is so great and yet so unattainable from the neglectful caregiver, the child begins to formulate a sense of self that is empty and forlorn. The child may come to believe she does not deserve her parents' love and affection, and the harder she attempts to earn this love, the more her self-esteem is eroded. As this negative cycle of seeking love and being rejected repeats itself, the feelings of negative self-worth solidify. These feelings may not necessarily be conscious in the early years; however, this is the period in which emotional memories are hard-wired in the developing brain. The negative beliefs about self and others are formed and cemented in the child's neurons. Neglect of the child leads to the child's feeling unlovable, and this emotion can be carried by the child into adulthood. Low self-worth, depression, and anxiety become a foundation for both the child and the developing adult's relationships with self and others.

Powerful feelings of low self-worth and depression can lead to thoughts of death and suicide, both in childhood and in adulthood. Indeed, depression is one of the leading symptoms of the suicidal person. Overt suicidality may not develop in the child until later years; however, many young people who have unrecognized, untreated depression can experience suicidal thoughts and feelings. Some children may even attempt to take their own lives. These suicide attempts often go unrecognized by the adults around them. The attempts may be disguised in the form of what can appear to be accidents. For example, a young child who consciously puts himself in the path of a moving car or truck may be mistaken for having done so by accident. Children may seek to escape pain and abuse at home in many ways. They may use strategies of compliance, avoidance, or more dramatic gestures of self-destruction. Some of these self-destructive acts may not be intended to cause death; rather, they may be a matter of caring so little that the child's risk-taking becomes dangerous, even lethal. Other examples of these types of behaviors include jumping off bridges, using substances, playing dangerously close to machinery, riding a bicycle at high speeds in dangerous traffic, and even playing with unattended weapons left in the home. Self-destructive acts by children may be impulsive and can be either conscious or acted out without conscious thought.

Heredity can also play a significant role in an individual's development of suicidal thoughts and behaviors. As discussed earlier in this chapter, biological seeds begin to be transmitted from parent to child in utero. Genes for mental health issues such as schizophrenia, bipolar disease, depression, and suicidality can be passed through the generations, along with the color of the infant's eyes, the shape of the child's face and body, and other physical attributes. Thomas Joiner explains that suicidal behaviors run in families, and that this is related to genetics, neurobiology, and personality traits. Genetics create a part of the foundation upon which the individual will develop; the environment adds to this foundation and can have either a positive or negative influence on the biology of the child. Family studies give evidence of the role of genetics in those who attempt or complete suicide, and twin and adoption studies clearly show that genes are involved in suicidal behavior.

Brain chemistry may also have an effect on a child's predisposition for depression and suicidality. Serotonin is a biochemical in the brain that helps regulate mood and emotion. Low levels of serotonin can cause depression and potentially lead to suicidality. A single gene, located on chromosome 17, is responsible for encoding the serotonin transporter gene. If this gene is compromised, low levels of serotonin can result. When such faulty genes are passed through familial bloodlines, low levels of serotonin can also be shared from generation to generation, from parent to child. Family biology and heredity can be responsible for a weak transporter gene and subsequent low levels of serotonin. Low levels of this substance in the brain alone, or compounded by a poor environment, can affect the positive development of self. Feelings of low self-worth that are generated in the home will be more difficult for the individual to overcome without necessary levels of serotonin to keep mood stable.

Cultural factors and the collective unconscious may also influence the developing self and suicidal tendencies. In some ethnic groups the numbers of completed suicides run much higher than in other ethnic groups; this may be a result of genetics, environment, learned patterns within the group, or the impact of the privileged culture on the smaller, underprivileged culture.

Consider the child who is raised in a Third World village in which several of the adolescent males and young men have completed suicide. In some Third World countries the village is like a large family and any loss impacts each member of the group. The male child raised in this village unconsciously carries knowledge that suicide is a familiar way that families have lost their sons to death throughout the history of their people. In this culture there may be a deep and long-standing sadness that is unspoken and carried by each village member. As the Western world impacts this culture, developing acculturation issues, as well as alcoholism, may compound the feelings of loss and lead to further suicides in the village. An example of this type of culture can be found in the Pacific Islands. The rate of suicide for young men in these islands is astronomically high. As the generations in this culture pass, depression and suicidal predisposition are transmitted from one family member to the next through genetics and cultural norms. Many young boys may have lost an older brother or uncle to suicide. As these boys reach the teenage years and are faced with alcoholism and the impact of Western culture, their sense of self is in doubt. They have witnessed their older family members die to suicide. They witness their cultural ways of life being impacted by industrialism but may have no means to join the new culture without feeling they are abandoning or disrespecting the older cultural traditions. The Western world has introduced alcohol, and their systems react to the substance as if it were poison. They quickly become addicted. When intoxicated, they become self-destructive and often complete suicide. The village mourns their youth. These young lives are lost to unconscious ghosts of long ago.

In the smaller urban nuclear family there may also be a long history from generations past of completed suicide. Stories of a great-great-grandfather who shot and killed himself may be passed down from mother to child. This same family may also include an aunt or uncle who took his or her own life, or a series of family members who have died by suicide. In some families and cultures, the completed suicide(s) may not be discussed; however, the feelings of loss can be passed unconsciously through the years. One family member's suicide may be the precursor to another's suicide many years later.

Similar to depression and other forms of mental illness, alcoholism can be passed through generations of cultures and families. When alcohol is used by an individual who is already depressed, it can create a deadly combination for death by suicide. Suicide attempts, suicide gestures, and completed suicides often occur when a depressed person is intoxicated. For individuals with poor impulse control, the use of alcohol or drugs lowers inhibitions and may propel the person to act without much forethought. When an intoxicated person who has thoughts of self-harm also has the means handy to kill herself, the risk is great for completed suicide. Substances may also provide the individual who has had thoughts of suicide the false bravado to actually act on her intent. Even when these individuals reach out for help, it can be difficult for those who may wish to intervene to stop the deadly course of events.

Genetic mental illness, substance abuse, culture, and environmental factors can all contribute to the development of the self. It is clear that the infant and developing child have little control regarding the state of matters in their early lives. Some lucky children may be born and raised in a family in which the gene structure is not laced with mental illness or addiction and the home environment is warm, loving, and privileged. However, other children begin at a disadvantage by inheriting compromised genes from their biological parents and by being raised in a home or culture with many emotional challenges to overcome. Some children are born into familial or ethnic cultures with long, multigenerational histories of suicidal behaviors; some are not. The child is not responsible for the family or culture he is born into or the biology he inherits. However, he must somehow find or be presented with the resources to function with what he is given. The following chapter will discuss how the early formation of trends toward suicide in childhood can impact the adult. Chapter 3 will address the way the individual can survive and flourish, even with beginnings that are laced with multiple challenges of biology, environment, and culture. Many adults have been able to take their adversities and use them to their advantage. The travails of the child raised with the challenges of a compromised family heredity, neglectful or abusive caregivers, or a culture comprising multigenerational suicides can be overcome. The resiliency of the human spirit is remarkable, and with courage and fortitude many obstacles can be mastered and redefined.

There are many interventions that can be useful in assisting a child who may begin life with genetic or environment challenges. It is especially important that adults be aware that each developing soul needs to be considered special and cherished. Caregivers may not be aware how much power they have in molding the life of a child and the lasting impact that their intervention can have in later years.

The following are early signs of suicidal tendencies to watch for in childhood:

- Crying often
- Moodiness or extreme emotionality
- Isolation
- Being overly quiet
- Not eating or overeating
- Drawing dark, sad, or violent pictures
- Trouble sleeping
- Talking about death
- Talking about "not wanting to be here"
- Wishing to be in heaven
- Acting out/aggression
- Impulsivity or dangerous acts, such as playing with fire or running into traffic
- Lack of play or spontaneity

Caregivers can thwart the development of suicidal tendencies in infancy and early childhood by the following behaviors:

- Creating a loving and nurturing environment for the infant and child
- Eating and sleeping well; ensuring the child eats and sleeps well
- Limiting the use of substances
- Touching the infant and child often and with love
- Playing with the child
- Listening
- Creating consistency in routines
- Limiting stress in the environment
- Playing soothing music
- Laughing
- Showing affection
- Asking the child what she worries about and listening carefully; showing care and concern for the child's concerns
- Providing positive responses to behaviors
- Limiting negative responses
- Removing harmful toys and creating an adult "watch" if there are concerns that the child may harm himself with impulsive behaviors
- Letting the child know that the caregiver is there to help
- Spending extra time with the child
- Taking the child seriously and not ignoring words or behaviors that are warning signals (listed above)
- Taking the child to a professional counselor if the behaviors persist

- Seeking counseling if feeling overwhelmed or if there are questions about what should be done for the child

ELIZA'S STORY

Eliza is a nine-year-old, middle-class, white female who is brought to see a therapist by her mother, Bethany. Bethany reports to the therapist that Eliza has been coloring pictures of heaven and saying she would like to be "up there" with her puppy. Eliza's dog was hit by a car and killed several weeks earlier, and her mother explained to Eliza that the dog had gone to heaven. Before the puppy died, it had been the focus of Eliza's world. The puppy had slept with Eliza at night and followed her about the house during the day when Eliza was home from school.

In gathering a family history, the therapist learns Eliza is a quiet child with few friends. Eliza is described as spending a lot of her time alone in her room drawing. Eliza's mother reports that she and her husband separated the previous year. Prior to the separation, there had been a lot of arguing in the home, and Bethany admits that both parents drank too much alcohol. Eliza's father had left the house after an especially bad argument and had not returned. Eliza has not talked much about her father moving out, even though Bethany has asked repeatedly how Eliza feels. Since the separation, Eliza's father has been visiting her once a month on Saturday mornings.

Eliza's mother reports that Eliza is eating and sleeping well and that she has not seen Eliza crying, even when the dog was killed. To Bethany's knowledge, there is no family history of depression or suicidality in her own family or in her ex-husband's family. Bethany states that she started to become worried about Eliza soon after the puppy had been killed and Eliza had asked many questions about heaven and what it is like there. Eliza had also asked Bethany if she would go to heaven if she got run over like her puppy. Soon her drawings had taken on similar images of sky and light and a puppy and a girl on a cloud. Eliza had told Bethany that the girl in the picture was herself. Eliza's father thinks that Bethany is making too much of Eliza's pictures and statements. Bethany, however, tells the counselor that she is alarmed because Eliza seem to be preoccupied with heaven and even wants to be there with her dog.

There are several risk factors that lead one to conclude that intervention would be helpful for Eliza. She obviously is preoccupied with the loss of her puppy and with thoughts of death and heaven. Eliza's mother is astute enough to realize that Eliza needs help and to take her daughter seriously when she says that she would like to be in heaven with her puppy.

Eliza's behaviors include the following risk signs for depression/suicidal predisposition:

- Wanting to be in heaven
- Pictures of herself in heaven
- Isolation
- Lack of friends
- Parental separation
- Loss of contact with her father
- Limited interaction with her mother/family
- Loss of beloved pet
- Possible low self-esteem
- Arguments between parents
- Substance abuse of parents

Eliza exhibits significant risk factors for depression. She is isolated and has little social contact with same-age friends, which is a developmental milestone for her age range. It appears that she has no close playmates either at school or at home. This social isolation may affect her self-esteem as other children around her surely are involved in activities that are age-appropriate. Compounding the social isolation, Eliza comes from a home in which there has been turmoil between her parents and then the sudden loss of the intact family system. It seems that there had been little discussion or explanation for Eliza when her father left home. Her contact with him had decreased immediately and had become limited. Eliza had then experienced the loss of her beloved pet, perhaps the one contact for her that had always been loving and consistent. There is some question of substance abuse by Eliza's parents, which could impact their ability to develop strong attachments to Eliza. Additionally, Eliza's father minimizes her symptoms. In her way, Eliza appears to be telling a story through her pictures of how she wants to die and be in heaven with her puppy.

The good news in this family is that Eliza's mother is taking both her daughter's verbal and nonverbal cries for help seriously. Bethany had become concerned and called a professional when Eliza had stated that she wanted to be in heaven with her puppy. In response to concerns like these, the counselor could provide an evaluation for Eliza to determine levels of depression and safety. The therapist could also design a treatment plan to assist Eliza and her family in identifying and implementing methods of recovery. Several therapeutic strategies could be utilized to help Eliza feel better about herself and her life. First, the therapist would engage Eliza and help her to begin to verbally express some of the angst she was feeling.

Eliza's art could act as a catalyst for this communication. The therapist would also engage Eliza's father in the treatment and help him to see that his daughter is, indeed, experiencing feelings of deep sadness and loss. Ideally, increased visitation would be arranged between father and daughter, and Bethany's one-on-one time with Eliza would also be increased. The therapist would teach Eliza coping strategies and social skills while working with her parents to improve their parenting skills. The counselor could provide resources for parenting classes of divorced couples and education regarding substance abuse and its impact on the family. Overall, Bethany's intervention of bringing Eliza to counseling could have a dramatic positive effect on Eliza and the family system.

The following methods of repair are recommended:

- Begin talk/play counseling for Eliza with a professional
- Increase consistent weekly visits with father
- Increase positive time/interactions with mother
- Increase positive reinforcement from parents (to improve sense of self)
- Increase social time with peers (play dates)
- Consider same-age counseling group participation
- Limit arguments between parents, especially in front of Eliza
- Create awareness in parents of substance abuse impact on Eliza
- Attend parenting classes for divorced couples

In her play therapy with her counselor, Eliza draws a picture of her family, which includes only her mother and herself. In the picture she draws herself very small in a corner. Her mother takes up most of the picture and is distant on the page from Eliza. Eliza's therapist is able to use the picture to help Eliza talk about her loneliness and fear. She does not understand why her father is gone from the home, and she misses him greatly. Eliza also has great fears that her mother will die. The therapist helps Eliza put words to her fears and facilitates direct communication between Eliza and her mother. Eliza's father is invited to a session with Eliza and her mother, and together they talk about the divorce and what it means to Eliza. Eliza's father also sets up more visitation time each week to spend with her.

While Eliza may not have been imminently suicidal, she certainly exhibited symptoms of depression. Without treatment Eliza's symptoms could have increased in severity, and eventually she may have become actively involved in gestures of self-harm or even suicidal. The process of becoming suicidal could have developed slowly or happened more quickly. In some cases with similar symptoms the depression does not develop into active suicidal intent. However, when a young child exhibits serious signs of depression that include talking about wanting to be in heaven (death), it is important to pursue an evaluation with a professional. Early intervention by Eliza's mother was instrumental in a number of ways. First, the fact that Bethany took notice and sought professional help provided Eliza with evidence that her mother cares about her and loves her. Second, Eliza was able, with the counselor's help, to put her sadness and fears into words and express them, rather than keeping them internalized. Third, the family dynamics were altered by the therapist's recommendation that both father and mother spend more consistent quality time with Eliza. Eliza was able to experience her needs being met in a very reparative manner.

IN CONCLUSION

The seeds for predisposition to suicidal tendencies may begin even in the womb. Genetics, environment, culture, temperament, and fate all play a part in creating both vulnerabilities and resiliencies in the infant and child. Each vulnerability factor, or a combination of factors, may put the developing person at a disadvantage for well-being, both in the present and in later years as an adult. The earlier that an intervention can occur the better. If mental health issues can be identified at an early age, skills can be developed within the family to help with change and adaptation. Then, in later life some learned skills will already be in place to manage the challenges that life presents. Without early intervention, the problematic issues can continue to grow and fester; they may combine with new issues relating to the environment and the developmental stage of the individual. However, with help, understanding, and intervention, suicidal action can be averted. There is hope.

2

---•❖•---

The Development of Suicidal Thought as We Age

> . . . the house is narrow, the place is bleak
> Where, outside wind and rain combine . . . with a malice . . .
> O enemy sly and serpentine.
> Do I hold the past
> Thus firm and fast
> Yet doubt if the future hold I can?
>
> Robert Browning

CASE EXAMPLE: A LEARNED RESPONSE

Rebecca had good insight. She could see that she was in yet another abusive relationship, and that it was a pattern for her. All the boys on the planet could not possibly be so cold and hard. She wondered if she was a magnet for those who didn't want a caring relationship. The boys she had been involved with seemed to use her, take advantage of her kindness, and then leave her. Some of them were verbally abusive. One of them frightened her half to death when he threw a lamp at her wall and then threatened to hit her with it. Most of them dated her a short while and then met other girls and moved on, leaving her behind.

Rebecca had hoped that her most recent relationship, with Jim, would last forever. Jim seemed to be a good match for her, and Rebecca thought he was someone who would want to be in a long relationship with her.

She went out of her way to buy him special little gifts, to send him cards, and to sometimes even bring his lunches for him. She sometimes did his homework for him, and tried not to ask too much of him.

Jim would often go out with his friends and leave Rebecca home on Friday and Saturday nights. He wouldn't return her text messages or calls, and he would make promises that he did not keep. Rebecca liked that she could tell others that she was in a relationship, and that she could be sure she would have a date for her senior prom that year. She did feel badly that he did not take her out much, or do thoughtful things for her. Jim also did not introduce her to his friends or to people at his job. This began to make her feel insecure, and she tried to find ways to "run into him" so that she could meet the people that he knew. Jim would call her too "needy" when she asked why he didn't return her texts or want to spend more time with him.

After eight months had passed, Rebecca began to hope that Jim would talk about their future together and perhaps begin to double date with some of his friends. She wanted to know that someone would love her and always be there for her. All of her girlfriends had guys that took them out, showed them off, and seemed to be attentive to them.

When Jim told her he didn't want to go out with her anymore, she hit her bottom. It was just before her senior prom, and he had met another girl. Although he would not admit that was the reason he was leaving her, Rebecca knew. Rebecca and Jim had been together for almost a year, and she was heartbroken and simply wanted to die. She didn't want to be alone anymore; she felt unlovable and worthless. She could barely force herself to get up in the morning to go to school, and she stopped eating. She fantasized about walking in front of traffic.

One night, she picked up the telephone book and looked under counselors. She knew she was in crisis and had to do something, so she started to make calls. She left many messages on therapists' answering machines, and several of them did not even call her back. The counselors that Rebecca spoke to were booked and not taking new patients. One or two of the counselors spoke with her at some length, and were kind and gave her referrals to call. Rebecca couldn't believe that she couldn't even find a counselor willing to meet with her. Finally, Rebecca decided to go to the school counselor's office. When she walked into the office for the first time, Rebecca couldn't stop crying. She couldn't talk. She just cried. The counselor was patient and sat with her, and scheduled another appointment with her for that same week.

The school counselor helped Rebecca to get connected to an outside therapist that she could see as much as she needed. Through her therapy,

Rebecca came to understand that she had been raised in a home in which her father was preoccupied with his business. He traveled often and was seldom at the dinner table. He never attended Rebecca's important events as she grew up. Looking back, Rebecca could almost feel the indifference that emanated from her father; until she began counseling she had not realized that her father suffered from clinical depression and had trouble engaging with his children any more than superficially. Rebecca's mother was kind and full of laughter; however, she was preoccupied with her own friends and enjoying her own life. Rebecca came to realize that she had never felt like she could ask for anything from her parents. She went along pretending that her life was fine even when she suffered from little girl hurts and teenage needs. Rebecca had teenage acne, which made her feel self-conscious and shy; she just never felt good enough for others and found herself spending a lot of her time reading books and in her room daydreaming. Rebecca could recall one poignant snapshot from her first year in high school that seemed to capture her feelings of aloneness. She had gone to a New Year's Eve party a few blocks from her house, and as it neared midnight all the girls had partnered off with boys except Rebecca. She felt awkward and uncomfortable, and knew that she would not be missed by her friends, so she walked the few blocks home. Her parents were having a party themselves. It was freezing cold outside, but Rebecca could not bring herself to walk into the house to the questions her parents would ask about her being home early. She sat on the snow-covered, icy steps and watched the adults count down to midnight through the window. They all seemed so happy and it was clear they felt that they belonged. Rebecca felt lost, alone, and out of place. She waited another 20 minutes in the cold and then tried to sneak past her parents' company to her own room upstairs.

When Rebecca was a junior in high school she felt actively suicidal for the first time. In her earlier years she had often pondered the meaning of life and death, and there were many times that she wished she would just not wake up. This time, however, Rebecca sat in her parents' kitchen and used a steak knife to make sharp cuts on her arm. She wondered what drugs she could take from the medicine cabinet that would kill her. One of her friends called and interrupted her actions. Rebecca never made any other active gestures of self-harm in the following years, but often wondered about the reason for her living.

During her therapy following her senior year, Rebecca came to learn that she had a distorted belief system that had been created during her childhood. In part, the belief system was unconscious, but became played out in her young adult life. Rebecca's primary caregivers did not have the time or attention for her, so as a young child Rebecca came to believe that she must be unlovable. She thought that if she was quiet and "good" and took care of others, her parents would love her love her more. She thought that if she just did more around the house and did not complain, someone would finally notice her and provide her with the love and attention that she craved. As Rebecca grew up and entered young adulthood, she played out this scenario again and again in her friendships and with boys she dated. She would give herself fully in her relationships and not ask for anything in return. When others would not respond to her or leave her, she would always ask herself, "What's wrong with me?" Despondency would then set in as Rebecca felt the hopelessness of being alone.

Rebecca's insight from her therapy helped her to see that her patterns of giving more and more of herself did not work. Her relationship with Jim provided Rebecca with the clear evidence that the more she gave, the less he appreciated her and the more she felt helpless. Although Rebecca could not see it at the time, Jim's abandonment provided her with an opportunity to look deeply at her core patterns and make changes that could lead her to healthier, more fulfilling relationships. As Rebecca learned not to give so much of herself away and to ask for what she needed, her relationships became more satisfying. While Rebecca had insight and could see the ineffective patterns she had engaged in, they were difficult to change. It took time, practice, and work in her therapy to overcome her old ways of reacting. Evidence of positive outcomes when Rebecca would have small successes helped her to continue to slowly change. She felt more hopeful, less helpless, and over time Rebecca established a sturdy relationship with a boy in college who shared life's challenges. Years later, when she looked back at her relationship with Jim, Rebecca could directly relate her choices to her early childhood.

CORE PATTERNS

The early years in the life of each individual set the foundation for the formation of the young adult and the mature adult self. As the child grows, her home environment sets a mold, and the adult steps out of this molded cast and into the world. Some of the life responses of the adult who has been raised in a home where there has been a cast set for suicidal tendencies, such as internalized despondency, learned helplessness, and rage, will be discussed in this chapter. The symptoms and behaviors of the suicidal adult are complex and designed from the unique factors of the individual's upbringing, heredity, and internal constitution. There is not one simple pattern but a constellation of issues that can be identified. Each individual makes meaning of her own existence in a manner that is her own, and the following pages are meant only to provide an illustration of some of the many ways that the adult may translate her pain into a self-destructive act. It is the hope that if some of the signs and symptoms of adult suicidality can be recognized in their earliest forms, completed suicide can be averted by interventions that will be noted later in this chapter.

Internalized Despondency, Learned Helplessness, and Rage

The combination of internalized despondency, learned helplessness, and rage, or one of these factors alone, can create a miserable existence for any human being. These feelings contribute to low self-worth, lack of pleasure in life, depression, hopelessness, and/or destructiveness. They limit the abilities of the healthy adult and can create significant impairment in daily functioning. Individuals experiencing long-standing despondency, feelings of helplessness, or rage have relationships with significant others that can be dramatically impacted in adverse ways. These individuals do not have the emotional energy to create and maintain levels of intimacy that are needed for a healthy adult relationship, or they use what energy they have to act out in destructive ways. Therefore, they may often find themselves isolated or in a relationship that is unrewarding or abusive. They may become victims, believing that this is all the world has in store for them. In school or at work, the despondent, helpless, or vengeful individual may not reach his potential or fulfill his basic responsibilities. His peers, colleagues, and supervisors can come to disdain his continued inability to function fully or his disruption of the school or workplace. Many times an inverted cycle of negative responses is created in which the despondency, helplessness, or rage leads to failure. This failure then manifests into greater despondency, helplessness, and anger, once again proving to the individual that he is, indeed, worthless.

Despondency

Internalized despondency is a deep-seated belief that there is no hope or help in the world; it is one of a constellation of symptoms that, if left untreated, can eventually lead an individual to clinical depression. A despondent adult who has come to have a core belief that there is little hope of positive experiences plods through life finding little joy or pleasure even in small things.

The despondent person may feel as if she has sandbags attached to each foot; each movement and action can take an incredible amount of effort.

Sleep and appetite may be disrupted, and thoughts may cycle in a nega-tive vortex in the despondent person's mind. Sadness may accompany the despondency; anger may also be present, but the energy to fulfill angry fantasies is generally not available to the person who is despondent.

In some cases, despondency may be the beginning of clinical depres-sion; in other cases, despondency may be one of a constellation of symp-toms that are the result of an already present biologically induced depression. In yet other cases, despondency may be environmentally car-ried from childhood or a reaction to an unresolved life tragedy.

When despondency is the result of biological factors that lead to clini-cal depression, there can be symptoms such as sleep disturbance, appetite changes, ruminating thoughts, and loss of interest in pleasurable activi-ties. The despondency that leads to a depressive episode may be triggered by a traumatic event, such as the loss of a loved one, a car accident, or any other tragic circumstance. Biological despondency and subsequent clini-cal depression may also surface without an environmental cause. As the length of time that an individual experiences her symptom(s) increases and she does not receive treatment, the despondency and depression can deepen.

Despondency that is carried from childhood may be a pervasive part of an adult individual's personality. This despondency may have been the way that the child survived a difficult childhood; that is, by shutting down and minimizing reactions to his home environment. It could also have been a learned emotion from his caregiver's responses to the world. The child has learned to mimic the adult and unconsciously seeks the same attention or secondary gains his parent received from being maudlin. These learned traits can be difficult to identify and alter in later life as they have been mechanisms that the individual uses to function and feel safe in his early years.

Despondency alone or in a cluster of other symptoms that result in clinical depression can lead to suicidal thoughts and behaviors. Living under a dark cloud for a long period of time diminishes the ability to be-lieve that life can have pleasure. Negative thoughts and low self-worth may drive the wish for life to end. Edwin Shneidman said, "Psychological pain is the basic ingredient of suicide. Suicide is never born out of exalta-tion or joy; it is a child of the negative emotions." The individuals for whom a primary feeling is despondency simply want to end the psycho-logical pain they are experiencing. Suicide may present them with the only option they can see; it may be a means to feel some control over a destiny that otherwise looms ahead as large and black. The despondent person often can see no other way out of the pain she is experiencing. If she has carried the heavy load of sadness and pain for many years, death may appear to be an oasis of peace and calm, beckoning like water in the desert. For the person who is experiencing overwhelming sadness from the loss of a loved one or a recent traumatic event, death may appear to be the only way for her to resolve her hurt. She is unable to see clearly through the deep pain of loss to find other options or a glimmer of hope. These individuals want only to stop the hurt, and often the only way they can see that will end their pain is to end their own lives.

While despondency may be created by deeply ingrained beliefs about the self, these beliefs can be altered. The thoughts, or cognitions, that make up negative beliefs and thoughts about oneself can be worked with and changed. The negative thoughts that are embedded in an individual's psyche may be tenacious; however, once they are recognized, they can be identified each time they occur. Once the thoughts are identified, they can be replaced with positive self-talk. The process of changing deeply ingrained beliefs requires time and hard work. Imagine the mind as a tape that has been set with a single set of negative messages that have been replayed again and again for years. Erasing the negative messages may be difficult because they are embedded in the rehearsed tape. However, with practice and repetition the messages can be rewritten and new, hopeful messages can be imprinted on the tape. Once a new set of positive messages are designed and become repetitive for the individual, she or he will slowly come to believe the new words. There may be times that the individual falls back in to the familiar negative ways of thinking, but over time these events will become the exception rather than the rule.

Helplessness

Learned helplessness, as its phrase indicates, is a feeling of powerlessness that originates from repeated attempts to gain mastery (success) and control that fail. Learned helplessness is not a biological phenomenon; rather, it comes from circumstances present in the environment. Continued feelings of helplessness may eventually join with a cluster of other symptoms to create a biologically engineered clinical depression. However, by itself, the feeling of helplessness originates from continued oppression in the environment.

Adults who have been raised in families who are from underrepresented populations may experience the feeling of learned helplessness. These individuals are not a part of the mainstream privileged white majority and can experience prejudice simply because of their skin color or nationality. These underrepresented adults have learned from an early age that they

are different and at risk of rejecting or violent behavior from others because they are not the same as the majority. Imagine an adult from a minority group standing at a bus stop with several people from the mainstream
culture. This adult may experience fear, anxiety, and helplessness as they
wonder if they may be confronted because they are different. Individuals
from the mainstream population seldom have to worry about prejudice
and generally are not aware that the person of difference has concerns for
his/her well-being. The fears may arise from an experienced history of
abuse or be reactive to the present situation. Regardless, the helplessness
generated from being in a minority is real. Vigilance to the surroundings is
felt to be necessary to remain safe from possible threat. Other persons of
difference who may have experienced oppression from the majority culture include those individuals with physical handicaps, those who look
different, and those who live in poverty. Those belonging to the privileged
majority continue along without awareness that individuals of difference
are experiencing anxiety. This unawareness contributes to the underrepresented persons' feelings of invisibility, isolation, and fear.

Similar to those from underrepresented populations, a white, privileged
child who is abused may feel helpless to stop the abuse in their environment; this abused child goes unseen and unheard as the adults around
them betray them with violence. When abused children of any culture or
nationality grow into adulthood, these early feelings of helplessness can
continue. For example, the adult may choose relationships in which his
needs are not met and feel helpless to change the pattern. Oftentimes for
these adults a repetitive life pattern exists in which they unconsciously
choose partners or employment in which they become victims of abusive
others. The helpless individual may reenact his early years in the hopes of
mastering the past; however, without intervention, the familiar dynamic
of abuse takes over, and feelings of helplessness remain and grow. It is
much like a moth being drawn to a flame. According to Roberta Satow,
"Freud believed that repetition compulsion was an unconscious drive toward self-destruction and a reflection of the death instinct. Most psycho-
analysts have rejected the concept of the death instinct and believe these
repetitive behaviors were originally adaptive and necessary for the child's
psychic survival, but in adulthood they are self-destructive." This is not to
say that the adult survivor of childhood abuse or the adult from an underrepresented population wants to feel helpless or abused; rather, old familiar patterns may unconsciously take over and life events become played
out to match early experience.

Learned helplessness is a state, much like despondency, that can lead to
suicidal thoughts and feelings. As the adult feels trapped in an abusive life

cycle and can see no way out, suicide can provide him with a choice and a feeling of control. For the helpless individual, the thought of suicide may be not only for escape; suicide may be viewed as a manner in which to "punish" the perpetrators or to gain the ultimate attention and power. This can be a magnetic fantasy; the helpless person may believe that he can finally have the last say. As the helpless adult feels more and more exhausted by his life of being a victim, he comes to understand that he can exert a lasting blow on the perceived "abusive others" by killing himself. The thought of this power becomes more and more seductive until the adult who feels helpless becomes moved to inflict self-harm.

The feelings of being helpless that have been created over time are not a fate that is locked in to a person's personality. While there may be some effects of hard-wired patterns in the brain from early exposure to abuse, these patterns can still be altered. With the help of a therapist to identify patterns and implement change, the individual can move to more effective functioning in the world. A therapist can assist this person in identifying healthier relationships and a safer living environment. For the person from a minority culture, the reality is that there may not always be safety in the environment. However, there may be strategies and ways to navigate the world that can be identified to make life less threatening.

Rage

Despondency and learned helplessness are reactions to life circumstances that become internalized by the individual. Rage is yet another reaction to negative life circumstances that develops internally but is manifested externally, either against the self or others. The child whose needs have been thwarted or who has been abused or ridiculed may develop into an adult with a grudge against the world. This adult's sense of self has been distorted through words and actions of early caregivers, and the reaction may be to strike back. This adult may seek to punish others through her own acts of abusive behaviors. As a child, this person was very likely unable to express any form of healthy anger for fear of punishment from the caregiver. The feelings of anger were suffocated, and the child was left to experience feelings of injustice and stifled, long-standing internalized rage. As this child moves into adulthood, the internalized rage may become safer to express and is externalized. This is extreme rage; the years of holding the anger inside have left the adult with no skills to modulate the intense emotion. The anger that spills out is generally disproportionate to the circumstance and frightening to the person receiving the furious reaction.

Externalized pervasive rage erodes the adult's relationships and, subsequently, any potential for positive self-regard. As the uncontrolled eruptions of anger destroy the adult's home life, work relationships, and friendships, this person may wallow in self-loathing. Samuel Vaknin said, "The first layer of anger, the superficial anger, is directed at an identified target, the alleged cause of the eruption. The second layer, however, is anger directed at himself. The patient is angry at himself for being unable to vent normal anger, normally. He feels like a miscreant. He hates himself." Anger can be the result of an abusive or neglectful early home environment. It can also be experienced by those from minority groups who have lived with oppression as a child and/or experienced violence or hatred as a result of their difference. Learned helplessness may translate into rage as the years unfold and the child becomes an adult.

As might be imagined, rage may be accompanied by a plethora of other emotive states. Self-loathing, self-pity, remorse, despondency, and jealousy complicate the enraged person's emotional state(s). Clinical depression may also be present, and suicidal and/or homicidal thoughts and actions may begin to take on a deeper role in the angry person's fantasies. This can be a very dangerous person as the anger is often impulsive, and if it is present in combination with drug or alcohol use, the result may be lethal. Unfortunately, the world has witnessed many acts of violence in which a raging individual has killed others and then committed suicide. Some of these acts are premeditated, well thought out, and planned. Other times they happen in moments of impulsivity or intoxication. According to the Violence Policy Center, approximately 1,500 deaths in the United States occur each year as a result of murder-suicide. Murder-suicide is particularly tragic in that it generally involves more than one victim and may involve a family with children.

Suicide may be the only option that the rage-filled person is able to see following an act of violence towards others. The latest episode of anger may have been one in a series from which he can finally see no other way out. Killing himself may be seen as the only way to stop the violence he perpetrates or the single action that can stop the feelings of shame he experiences.

The angry person may also feel that she can "punish" others by taking her own life. For example, if a romantic relationship or a position of employment has ended against the enraged person's wishes, she may decide to "show" the other person(s) what they have done and kill herself in an impulsive act of retribution. Similar to the despondent and helpless person, the rage-filled person may not realize that she has options other than suicide.

Rage is an emotion that is born from circumstance, entwined in events that include the actions of others and the reaction of the angry individual. While the actions of others may not be under control of the individual, the response of anger can be changed. The shift from rage to a healthier response takes insight, awareness, and a willingness to change. The individual that possesses these criteria for change can work with his/her support system and design a plan for addressing his/her anger. As the anger diminishes it is often found that there are a wealth of other feelings yet untapped within the angry person, awaiting attention and release. As the process of attending to these other feelings and needs are addressed, the individual's rage diminishes and a healthier self arises from the wreckage. A part of healing for the angry individual may be to make amends for the hurt they have caused others with their reactions. The journey to making amends may take time but marks the road to significant, healthy change.

Distorted Belief System

The person who attempts suicide has developed a strong negative belief system that may include several components. These beliefs have been internalized from an early age and are a powerful force that consumes the adult's thoughts and behaviors and can lead to suicidal intent. Distorted beliefs are cognitions that can become embedded in a person's thoughts. When a child is repeatedly told that they are bad, unattractive, and stupid or given any other negative message on a routine basis, they can come to internalize these messages. These internalized thoughts then become beliefs about the self.

Distorted beliefs of the suicidal adult can include the thoughts that she has no other option than suicide, she is powerless to stop the negative patterns in her life, and she will always feel despondent, helpless, or angry. These individuals may believe that they are a burden to others because of their negative impact on those closest to them. The belief that they cannot make changes and that their lives will be a continued cycle of the same miserable feelings propels them to want to end their days.

The suicidal person may harbor the belief that he has nothing to live for and that his days will continue on hopelessly, full of pain and without any measure of joy or happiness. Because his significant relationships have been impacted by his emotional state(s), this person may be isolated or surrounded by others who have also become weary of the distress he constantly experiences and projects. This isolation and rejection further impacts the suicidal adult and solidifies for him that there is nothing left for him. He feels exhausted and overwhelmed, and he cannot believe that tomorrow may be different.

Unfortunately, as stated earlier, the suicidal person can also have fantasies that her death will bring her sympathy or revenge. She may spend time imagining how the important others in her life will feel after she is dead. She may have the belief that her suicide will "teach" her family members, co-workers, and friends just how bad she was feeling or that suicide will show them how much she will be missed or how much she was misunderstood or mistreated. Her own funeral may be replayed in the suicidal person's mind with key players acting out the desired outcome of grief and anguish. This imagined drama provides some level of proof to the suicidal person that she is loved and will be longed for after she is gone.

Perhaps the most universal and destructive distorted belief of the suicidal person may be the belief that he is unlovable and that there is nothing he can do to change this fact. These feelings of unworthiness may be a core belief that started at a very young age when he was not nurtured and revered as a child. In adulthood, when this individual experiences fractured relationships, he can feel many of the same emotions that he did as a child. The feelings of being unlovable subsequently grow and solidify. Even the smallest rejection by another may trigger earlier feelings of abandonment or abuse and add to the pile of evidence the adult is compiling to prove that he is, indeed, not worthy. The suicidal adult takes the belief that he is unlovable and creates a more self-destructive belief that he will *never be loved*. He cannot see his way out of this faulty assumption; therefore, the future looms large and bleak. Many mental health issues arise from the underlying core belief of the adult that he is unlovable. Issues such as depression, anxiety, adjustment reaction(s), self-mutilation, and other factors that develop in reaction to the environment and upbringing can have devastating, long-standing effects that eventually may lead the individual to suicidality.

As with altering the negative feelings that accompany despondency, distorted thinking can also be changed. It can at times be difficult to determine whether distorted, negative thoughts come first for some individuals or begin with feelings of despondency that continue in a negative downward spiral. In some respects, it is not so important to make this distinction. Rather, the importance lies in changing the thoughts so that the individual can come to understand and believe that he/she is lovable and worthwhile. Cognitive behavioral therapy can be most helpful in altering negative thoughts, and the therapeutic relationship can provide an environment in which the individual can feel likeable.

HIGH-RISK FACTORS

Statistics show that there are several factors and multiple populations that are at highest risk for attempted or completed suicide. These factors and populations are noted below and are especially important in helping to recognize the suicidal adolescent or adult. Without knowledge of the signs to look for and the groups that may be most affected by suicidality, many suicidal individuals will not receive the help they need to avert death. There may be other factors and groups at high risk that are not listed below, but these are the most predominantly featured in the literature on suicide.

High-Risk Factors for Suicide:

- Mood disorders, particularly depression
- Other mental health disorders
- Substance abuse
- Low self-worth
- History of previous suicide attempts/hospitalizations
- Impulsivity
- History of physical/sexual abuse/disruptive behavior
- History of deliberate self-harm
- Opportunity (that is, easy access to firearms, etc.)
- Family history of suicide/mental health issues
- Serious medical illness

Populations at High Risk for Suicide:

- Adolescents
- Runaways/the homeless
- The elderly
- White men—for completed suicide
- Women—for suicide attempts
- Gay, lesbian, transgender, and gender-questioning individuals
- Native Americans
- Native Alaskans
- Pacific Islanders

According to the United States Preventative Services Task Force (USPSTF), risk factors for attempted suicide are mood disorders, co-morbid substance disorders, and a history of previous suicide attempts. Other risk factors that are noted include aggressive behavior and a history of physical or sexual abuse. The USPSTF reports that two-thirds of suicidal deaths occur on the first attempt, with higher completion rates for men than for women. Women may attempt suicide more often than men, but men use more lethal means and have a higher rate of success in killing themselves. More than 90 percent of the individuals who complete suicide are reported to have a psychiatric illness at the time of death, usually depression, alcoholism, or both. The USPSTF goes on to report that 75 percent of suicides are completed by white males. Caucasian males complete suicide twice as often as African American males. Native Americans are also suggested to be at high risk for suicide.

It is interesting to note that the most privileged group in society, the white male, has the highest rate of completed suicide. Marginalized groups such as the elderly, gays and lesbians, Native Americans, Pacific Islanders, and the homeless also are at high risk. Statistically, these marginalized groups have far less membership; therefore, the numbers that are based on volume may not correctly represent proper analysis of the data.

Additionally, alcohol and drug use is noted to be highest among the more marginalized high-risk populations listed above, such as Native Americans, Native Alaskans, Pacific Islanders, and the homeless. The use of substances may place an already high-risk individual in an even more vulnerable position. Intoxication leads to distorted thinking, increases depressive states, and can lead to impulsive behavior. The combination of substance use and already present suicidal intent or newly emerging suicidal thought may be disastrous.

INCREASING INCIDENCE: STATISTICS

The statistics regarding suicide are staggering and have increased significantly since the 1950s. Each number represents a person that might not have died had an intervention occurred or if someone had reached out to them.

- Suicide ranks as the third cause of death among young Americans between the ages of 15–24; suicide is the third leading cause of death among college students (in the United States only accidents and homicide claim more young lives).

- Youth suicide (ages 15–24) rates have increased significantly from the 1950s; between 1952 and 1995, suicide in young adults nearly tripled.
- Suicide takes the lives of 40,500 Americans each year.
- Worldwide, there are more deaths due to suicide than to accidents, homicides, and war combined.
- Suicide is the 10th leading cause of death in the United States.
- There are 110.9 suicides per day.
- There is one suicide every 13 minutes.
- 20 percent of American high school students report having seriously considered suicide during the previous 12 months.
- The strongest risk factor for suicide is depression.
- Early recognition and treatment of depression and other psychiatric illnesses appears to be the best way to prevent suicide.
- Many who attempt suicide never seek professional care.
- 80 percent of people that seek treatment for depression are treated successfully.
- Suicide rates in the United States are the highest in the spring.
- Substance abuse is a risk factor for suicide; 70 percent of youth who die by suicide are frequent users of alcohol/drugs.
- Males complete suicide at a rate 3.6 times that of females; however, females attempt suicide three times more often than males.
- Over half of all suicides occur in adult men, ages 25–65.
- Suicide rates are highest among those aged 45–54.
- 50.9 percent of suicides in 2012 used firearms; 24.8 percent used suffocation; 16.6 percent used poisoning.
- Males' method of choice is most often firearms; females' is most often poisoning.
- Suicide results in an estimated $34.6 billion in combined medical and work loss costs.
- Rates of suicide are highest in the Mountain states; the Northeast Atlantic states have the lowest.

Sources: American Association of Suicidology, *Suicide in the United States*, http://www.suicidology.org/Portals/14/docs/Resources/FactSheets/USA2012.pdf; Suicide Awareness Voices of Education (SAVE), *Suicide Facts*, http://www.save.org/index.cfm?fuseaction=home.viewPage&page_id=705D5DF4-055B-F1EC-3F66462866FCB4E6; American Foundation for Suicide Prevention, *The Truth about Suicide: Real Stories of Depression in College*, http://www.afsp.org/preventing-suicide/our-education-and-prevention-programs/programs-for-teens-and-young-adults/the-truth-about-suicide-real-stories-of-depression-in-college.

Traumatic events may also be a precipitant to suicidal thought or action. Some of these events can include the issues of relationship difficulties, such as a recent breakup or divorce; financial difficulties; loss of employment; major losses caused by events, such as a tornado, fire, earthquake, terrorist attack, etc. Any traumatic event that creates great distress can lead some people to feel that there is no way out other than suicide. Many of the warning signs for suicide are listed below, along with resources for the suicidal person and for the concerned other. It is important that the warning signs be taken seriously and that help be sought from a professional. Suicidal thought and intent is treatable, and if help is obtained, many suicidal people go on to lead happy, healthy, and productive lives.

SIGNS OF SUICIDALITY IN YOUNG AND MATURE ADULTHOOD:

- Disturbed sleep
- Loss of appetite or overeating; sudden weight change
- Crying
- Loss of interest/pleasure in activities
- Missed work
- Increased substance use
- Impaired relationships
- Thoughts of suicide
- Talk of wanting to die
- Giving away treasured items
- Increased moodiness/anger
- Fatigue
- Difficulty concentrating
- Decrease in sexual drive
- Isolation
- Interest in wills and insurance policies
- Increased energy/improved mood just prior to suicide attempt

WHAT TO DO IF YOU ARE EXPERIENCING SUICIDAL THOUGHTS OR FEELINGS:

- Talk to someone:
  - ✓ Relative or friend
  - ✓ Therapist (often listed in directories under "Counselors")
  - ✓ Spiritual or clergy leader
  - ✓ Health care provider

- ✓ Call the National Suicide Prevention Lifeline (1-800-273-TALK [8255]) to speak to someone immediately.
- Understand that suicidal thoughts and feelings are symptoms that CAN be helped/changed if you reach out.
- Avoid additional stress:
  - ✓ Comfort yourself with favorite, relaxing things such as a cup of tea, a warm bath, talking with a friend, grooming your pet, reading a novel, or watching a light comedy
  - ✓ Take the pressure off yourself. Don't set goals that may be hard to reach or put any additional responsibility on yourself
  - ✓ Surround yourself with people who are loving and supportive
  - ✓ Be gentle with yourself

WHAT TO DO IF YOU ARE CONCERNED THAT SOMEONE ELSE MAY BE SUICIDAL:

- Encourage the person to talk:
  - ✓ Listen
  - ✓ Ask questions
  - ✓ Let the person do most of the talking
  - ✓ Tell the person that things can change
  - ✓ Take the person seriously
  - ✓ Don't be afraid to talk about suicide; talking about it will not make it happen
  - ✓ If the suicidal person refuses help, remember that help is available for concerned persons (you) from a counselor.
  - ✓ Help the person make an appointment with a counselor and offer to accompany her or him to the visit if s/he wishes
  - ✓ If there is any concern of immediate harm, call 911

Concerned persons can call the National Suicide Prevention Lifeline (1-800-273-TALK [8255]) to get names of counselors in the area and to get assistance from a hotline therapist in how to talk to the suicidal person. It is important that concerned people do not take on the role of counselor themselves or feel that they can be the one to "rescue" the suicidal person. A professional will know the best way to help. Individuals concerned about someone else being suicidal also need help themselves in dealing with this dangerous situation. Do not try to manage it all alone.

The life responses to early childhood discussed in this chapter that can impact the adult and lead to suicidal thoughts are all treatable with professional help. The combination of cognitive therapy and medication has an extremely high rate of success for these individuals. For suicidal people who are reluctant to take medication, counseling can have a positive effect by itself in many cases; for those who are adverse to "talk" therapy, medication alone may also be successful. However, it is important to note that the highest rate of success is in individuals who combine counseling with medication.

Suicidality is a debilitating and complicated phenomenon with many faces, as shown in this chapter. It is tragic when there is a completed suicide because the symptoms, with help, can be reduced and, in many cases, eliminated.

The following chapter will explore the individual's weaknesses and strengths in managing suicidal thoughts and feelings. A person may emerge into young adulthood with many early predisposition factors for depression and suicide. However, the individual may also have internal and external resources for changing his or her own destiny.

3

❖❖❖

Our Weaknesses and Strengths in Fighting Suicidality

MAKING LEMONADE FROM LEMONS

Her MP3 player was so loud that others could hear the music as she walked through the gym. She had her eyes half-closed and was imagining herself as the singer. She could see herself on the stage with her backup band and the thousands of fans in the audience screaming her name. She knew every word of the song by heart, and there were times she had to consciously stop herself from singing them out loud. She imagined herself making eye contact with one of the boys in the imaginary band that was playing guitar. She liked to pretend that he was in love with her, and in her fantasy she would turn and sing to him when they would play the love songs. He would mouth the words back to her; they had a special bond.

While she moved through the gym listening to her music, she was at first unaware of the other girls who were watching her. When the song finished, she looked up and saw the three of them, and she knew they were laughing at her. She must have been singing out loud again. She felt her face flush in embarrassment and moved more quickly to reach the door. She didn't have any close friends at school and always felt like the popular girls were watching her and thinking she was weird. One of the girls stepped in front of her, and she thought she was going to cry.

She was 14 years old, and she just never felt like she belonged anywhere. Her father was in the service, and her family moved all the time. As soon as she felt like she was beginning to make friends in one place, her family would move again. At home, she and her mother were alone most of the time. Her father worked long hours on the base and sometimes was away on business for a week at a time. When he would come home, her parents would spend most of their time fighting; sometimes her father would hit her mother and threaten to hit her if she tried to help. She was afraid of her father and would spend time in her room when he was home. In her room she felt safe, and she could imagine a world in which she was the popular girl everyone wanted to have as their friend. She had a vivid fantasy life that included her music and special characters on her television shows. She would conjure up images of herself as the heroine and would hurry home to daydream. She would listen to her music or watch one of her shows and get lost in a world of fantasy.

She was always worried about her mother. She wondered what would happen to her if her mother were to get sick and die. There would be no one to take care of her. Her mother always seemed to be in another world and didn't pay much attention to her. She wished that she had a brother or sister to talk to, especially at night when she was most afraid. Once, she had come home and had found her mother on the floor in the kitchen; she had not known what had happened, but her mother would not wake up. She had run next door to get a neighbor, and they had called an ambulance. She had to stay with her neighbor overnight until her mother had come home. No one had ever told her what happened.

The girls at this school seemed worse than at other schools, where the kids would just ignore her. These girls seemed to want to pick on her, and she didn't have any idea what to do about it. When the girl stepped in front of her in the gym, she burst into tears. She felt afraid, alone, and trapped. She felt different and she believed that she would never belong anywhere because she was always new and didn't fit in with the crowd. One of the girls who blocked her way looked worried when she started to cry and told her friends to stop being bullies. The three girls let her pass, and she ran out of the gym into the school yard. She ran home, and no one was there, so she went into her room and turned on the music, getting lost in her daydreams and fantasies about being loved and popular.

This 14-year-old was raised in a home environment of neglect. Her father was often unavailable, and when he was at home, he was sometimes abusive to her mother. She often felt afraid of her father, and when he was home, she would stay in her room as much as she could. Her mother was often drunk or sleeping due to her alcohol use. The child was moved often and had few friends because her family never stayed in one place for very long. She was an only child and did not have a close extended family with whom she could build healthy, loving bonds.

This child found that she was often in the position of caring for herself. At an early age she had learned to dress herself and get ready for school. She was able to find what she needed to eat in the pantry when her mother slept late. Her emotional needs were never addressed by the adults in her life.

As the years went by, she had developed a coping mechanism of using fantasy to help ease her fear, sadness, and loneliness. When she was very young, she had played with her dolls, and as she got older, she lost herself in her music and fantasy. She liked to read and imagine herself as one of the characters in a happier place with a big family. Because depression can be a silent illness and she had not stayed in one place long enough for a teacher or other adult to notice that she was withdrawn, no one had intervened or reached out to her.

Looking back on her life she can remember always having felt very sad, except for when she was in her dream world. There were times when she learned from her parents that they were going to move once again when she would wish that she could just die instead of having to pack. She could clearly recall the incident when she was 14 years old and the girls in the new gym had tried to bully her. This was the first time that she had cut herself. These first cuts had not been deep, and she had covered the marks with long sleeves until they had healed. She used her fingernails or a sharp object, such as part of her pen, to make the cuts. As an adolescent, she continued to cut herself in places that no one would notice. Most of the time, she did not necessarily want to die, but she did want to inflict pain on herself. There were times, however, when she became so depressed that she did want to take her own life. She had a plan to leave a long note to her parents, telling them how much she hated her life and how much happier she would be if she could just go to sleep and not wake up. She knew her mother had medications she could take, and once she had taken a bunch of pills, but they had only made her feel sick to her stomach.

She moved into young adulthood with periods of dark depression that came and went. She stopped the cutting because she was ashamed of the scars, but she began to drink heavily. She became very attractive, and she had boyfriends, but they did not last. When she graduated and had a job there were many people that she could have developed relationships with, but she did not initiate this companionship. She continued to feel isolated and alone; it was as if her childhood followed her everywhere, and she could not change things. She continued to use her fantasy world as a place of safety and hope. She would put her thoughts into writing, and she had a number of journals going at any one time.

When she was 24 and living alone, she drank several glasses of wine and decided to drive to the beach. She knew she should not drive under the influence, but she didn't care. As she drove, she found herself going faster and faster and again having that feeling that she did not want to live anymore. She impulsively pushed her pedal to the floor, and as she rounded a tight corner, the car flew off the road and crashed into a tree.

She woke up in the hospital with a broken collarbone and serious bruising. She was angry that she was alive. She couldn't stop crying. The hospital staff soon realized that she didn't have visitors and that she seemed to be depressed, so they had the hospital social worker visit her. It was clear to the social worker that she was suffering from clinical depression, in addition to her medical trauma.

This was the beginning of her journey to recovery. The hospital social worker spent time with her in the hospital and helped her to put a name to the depression that she had been feeling all her life. She agreed to seek counseling when she was discharged. Her first several sessions were very uncomfortable for her because she had never been the focus of anyone's attention before and she hardly knew what to say to the therapist. After all, her parents had never hit her or been sexually abusive to her. She felt as though she must be making up her problems. Her counselor slowly helped her to see that she had been neglected and isolated all her life. The therapist helped her to begin to understand that neglect can be even more destructive than physical or sexual abuse because it is invisible and insidious. She was able to learn about her resiliencies with the counselor's help. She had survived; a plant with almost no water had grown in rocky soil. The counselor acted as the first mirror that she had ever had, and, as her therapist reflected herself back to her, she could begin to see herself in a positive light for the first time. She was referred for a trial of medication, and this, combined with her counseling, lifted her depression for the first time that she could remember. She began to use her fantasy world in a much more functional way by writing stories that she could publish, taking an early coping skill and building it into a second career. With the support of her therapist she joined a women's group and began to initiate social contacts with her colleagues. As she became educated regarding alcoholism and depression, she stopped her drinking completely and attended twelve-step meetings. Her resiliency grew as she utilized both old and new coping skills. She learned that if she felt suicidal or the urge to drink, these feelings were a new version of the earlier cutting she had done that was intended to cause herself pain.

Her vulnerabilities included parental neglect, possible biological predisposition to depression, genetic predisposition to alcoholism and later-life alcohol consumption, isolation, poor self-esteem, lack of familial and social supports, and her own depression, which was manifested in self-abusive behaviors and suicidality.

Her resiliencies included an active, positive fantasy life with music, writing, and daydreaming about a better life. She was also willing to seek counseling when it was offered, to build and utilize coping skills, and to stop alcohol consumption. While she had many vulnerabilities to suicidal predisposition, she also had several resiliencies and an internal survival instinct that could be built upon and fortified.

OUR WEAKNESSES AND HUMAN VULNERABILITIES TO ADULT SUICIDE

The development of suicidal thoughts and feelings can begin in the earliest stages of biological and personality formation, or they may emerge in one moment of great individual hopelessness or trauma. As discussed in Chapter 2, the people who can be most vulnerable to suicidal ideation may have family histories laced with depression, suicidal gestures, or completed suicide(s). These individuals may also have had early home environments in which they were abused or neglected. When interpersonal trust is violated at an early age, the victim can have great difficulty choosing later relationships that are well balanced and healthy. Unfortunately, a pattern can be established in which, according to Liz Grauerholz, early "victims may find themselves caught within social networks that are exploitive and that cause further reduction in the ability to trust others." These individuals may chose partners and significant others who are similar to the early caregivers who were unkind, ambivalent, or abusive to them, and are, therefore, familiar. As a cycle of negative life experiences continues from childhood into adulthood, hope for change in the future diminishes. These people may also find themselves isolating and using avoidance patterns in their interactions, creating further vulnerabilities to loneliness, depression, and suicidal thought. The early vulnerability factors that lead to adult depression and suicidality are powerful events to be overcome.

As the young child develops within his family and culture, his core being is formed. Impediments to a healthy, happy lifestyle are cultivated when the family of origin has biological/environmental hazards, such as medical illness and/or mental illness, or neglect or abuse toward the child.

The type of individual medical history that can compromise a child's well-being might include her own medical illness such as asthma, Lyme disease, leukemia, Crohn's disease, cerebral palsy, cancer, irritable bowel syndrome, congenital heart disease, or any other chronic or acute medical condition that impacts the child's daily functioning. These medical conditions may limit or interfere with the child's interactions with others, including family, friends, and schoolmates. School may be missed, and this can result in academic struggles, which, in turn, can affect self-esteem. If the child's family system does not know how to assist the medically challenged child, vulnerabilities can manifest and grow. Medical vulnerability can be significant in the breeding of depression. As the child experiences feelings of powerlessness and difference from others due to her medical challenges, she may internalize feelings of sadness and hopelessness that can lead to depression and suicidal thought. Children with medical illness may carry a great deal of guilt over requiring so much attention from the family. These children can come to believe that they are an emotional and financial drain on the family. While they are medically ill, they also may experience emotional difficulties that can linger long after the illness has passed. These children can feel shame that their bodies are different than others in their peer group; for example, a child with Crohn's disease or irritable bowel syndrome may often be in need of using the bathroom at inopportune times. The need to stop activities for a bathroom break can feel embarrassing to these children, who want to appear to be like everyone else. A child with a medical illness will naturally be more tired than other children as her body uses more of its resources to compensate for the disease. She may wish to play as her peers do and can feel left on the sidelines when her body does not cooperate. The psychological aspects of medical issues can have great adverse impact on a growing youngster and may create serious vulnerability for depression.

A family member's medical illness may also create vulnerabilities for depression in a child. When someone else in the family system becomes chronically or acutely ill, all attention may be focused on that person, and not on the growing child. For example, if the mother in the family has cancer, family life will be focused around getting the mother to office visits and caring for this parent. The children in the family may experience deep and possibly realistic fears that their mother could die. These children may become isolated and unnoticed amid the medical crisis of the other family member. When a parent is ill, the children can experience great fears that they may be left alone. Some of the fears can become reality when a parent is hospitalized and the child wonders if the parent will ever come home again. Compounding these fears, when one parent is ill, the other parent often focuses all attention on the sick partner and has few emotional resources left to help the children understand and cope. The children may be left to guess and wonder about their sick parent and not have a clear or realistic understanding of the process of recovery. If the parent dies from the illness, another trauma befalls them as they deal with this grief.

When a sibling has a medical illness, a similar scenario may take place. A sibling's medical illness can be complicated and create vulnerability for depression in its own way for the healthy child. The child who is well may feel survivor guilt that he has escaped the awful sickness that has consumed his brother or sister. At the same time, he may also fear that he could come down with the same illness that is harming his sibling. The healthy child may harbor some jealously that his sibling is getting all the attention, and he may feel guilty for having these feelings.

Familial medical illness can create vulnerability in children for depression in early life or in later life. The child may manage to get through the period in which the family member is ill without showing signs of impact. However, unless attention is provided to the needs of the child who remains well, there could be symptoms that emerge later in time for this person. It can be terribly traumatic for a young person to watch a loved one with a catastrophic illness. When any family member is sick, generally much of the energy in the family is directed to the person who is ill. Unless a family or other elder is wise enough to notice and address the needs of the healthy family members, vulnerabilities are apt to arise for these individuals at some point in time, especially the children.

Mental illness in a child's family may also lead to early tendencies for depression. At times, the symptoms for depression in reaction to familial mental illness may not manifest until later life, but the seeds may be sown early. Mental illnesses such as schizophrenia, bipolar disorder, Asperger's syndrome, obsessive-compulsive disorder, panic disorder, or a family member's depression can significantly impact a child's emotional state. The child may grow up in an environment in which she does not have consistency and does not know what to expect from the behavior of her parent or sibling. In some cases, such as with schizophrenia, the behavior of the mentally ill family member may be bizarre or even violent. Some schizophrenic individuals hear voices that tell them to kill themselves or others. Imagine being a child in a family in which one of the parents or a sibling continually talks to himself and speaks of violent images or yells at the child for no apparent reason at all. Further, imagine if the child in that home is routinely threatened by the schizophrenic person or told that the devil is coming to kill the whole family. The child will most likely feel terrified and confused. These children will love their family member, yet they will fear the mentally ill person as well. Children with family members who have mental illness are impacted emotionally. If they have a parent or sibling who is depressed, this can be as frightening in its own way as having a psychotic or schizophrenic family member. The child in the home with the depressed loved one may have heard threats of suicide and be fearful that her parent or sibling will commit suicide. The child may be witness to a parent staying in bed all the time or to a caregiver who self-medicates with alcohol or drugs. Mental illness in a family member can create vulnerability and depression in the child. Familial mental illness may also lay the groundwork for depression and emotional issues in later life, especially if the child's needs and fears are unrecognized during the event of the illness. Families with mental illness constitute a double-edged sword of vulnerability for the child; there is both the emotional impact created by the illness and the genetic predisposition that is inherent in any family member of the mentally ill.

Other vulnerabilities include familial physical abuse, sexual abuse, substance abuse, neglect, poverty, and racism. Clearly, each of these circumstances can have a profound impact on a developing child and create a legacy for issues such as poor self-esteem, anger, sadness, isolation, and fear. In turn, each of these issues may be a causal factor that leads to suicidal thought or intent.

Childhood vulnerabilities may lead the developing youngster to feelings of despondency and learned helplessness. The individual may develop into an adult who can see very little hope. Conversely, this adult may harbor deep feelings of rage and anger, which disrupt her ability to function in a healthy way in the world. As the negative cycle grows, the individual's responses to the world become based on the early environment that began in her family of origin.

Specific Vulnerabilities to Adult Suicidality:

- History of family physical illness
- History of family mental illness
- Child physical abuse
- Child sexual abuse
- Child neglect
- No "important other"
- Traumatic event
- Loss
- Disrupted relationships (divorce, multiple partners)

- Hopelessness/rage that impacts functioning
- Childhood mental illness/physical illness
- Early family conflict
- Low socioeconomic status
- Substance abuse/self or family member
- Exposure to racism
- Absence of parental supervision
- Use of age-inappropriate media

The developing self is very sensitive to the environment, and negative factors can be easily internalized. For example, being raised in a family that provides limited supervision and interaction may lead to the child's feeling unlovable. As the child comes to have a belief that he is not worthy of others' attention, he also may be filling up his knowledge of the world with the media's images of violence, sexuality, and a distorted idea of intimate relationships. If the child becomes focused on violent media images, he may internalize violence and believe that aggression is a proper behavioral response in his interactions with others. Isolation, feelings of worthlessness, anger due to caregiver ambivalence, and aggression reactive to media images can combine to create a powerful environment that can breed violence against self or others.

Conversely, if the isolated child is one who instead focuses on fantasy, her young mind may become laced with romantic images and a world that does not truly exist. Both the child who entertains himself with aggressive images and the child who watches fantasy have been left by their otherwise occupied caregivers to design their own set of beliefs about the world around them. None of these beliefs are based in full reality. These children may become vulnerable to acts of violence against others or self, or vulnerable to others who may prey on them. These vulnerabilities may lead to depression and suicidal thought or action.

A child who is raised in poverty is also vulnerable to depression and subsequent suicidal predisposition. This child may be raised in a home in which there is not enough to eat or the nutrition is not sufficient to promote proper body/brain function. The child may feel shame that his clothing is old and does not fit correctly; he may be cold and not have the needed outerwear to keep warm. There may be little or no electricity in the home to heat the building or to cook warm meals. Many of the privileges that most people take for granted can be elusive to those who live in poverty. Compounding the lack of resources, the impoverished child also may experience feelings of embarrassment and fear, and prejudice from others. The feelings of shame and need from early years of poverty can follow a child throughout his life, creating low self-worth and subsequent depression.

In a home in which there are unstable or multiple relationships between the adults, there can exist a sensation of disconnectedness or attachment disruption for the children who live there. As discussed in Chapter 1, violent relationships, including physical, sexual, and verbal abuse, can have both an immediate and long-standing impact on a child's emotional well-being. Children can be impacted by a parent who has multiple partners with whom they become attached and then lose. If this kind of significant loss occurs many times in a young person's life, she may come to believe that her parent's partners are leaving because of her. She may feel or believe that she is not lovable enough for the other adult to stay, and her self-esteem can be greatly impacted. When a child is raised in a single-parent home and the caregiver has multiple partners but does not recognize the impact that this can have on the child, vulnerabilities are created. These young people can become vulnerable to sadness and depression, triggered by repetitive loss.

Vulnerability for depression can also be created by a traumatic event in the life of a child or young person who has not yet developed the appropriate resources to cope with the event. Examples of traumatic events include tragic accidents in which there is death or serious injury, seeing a loved one being harmed or die, witnessing extreme violence, witnessing a friend drown, being abandoned, or being held without consent. There are many other kinds of trauma that can significantly impact a child's emotional well-being that may not initially appear to be as damaging as some others. However, any event or series of events that causes a negative ripple effect on a child can ultimately foster vulnerability for depression. For example, if a child loses a pet and then experiences the loss of a beloved grandparent, the combined events could potentially lead to despair.

Childhood vulnerabilities to depression are numerous and can have a lasting effect on both the child and her journey to adulthood. Although there are many ways in which an individual can become vulnerable, there are equally as many resources with which resiliencies to protect against vulnerabilities and resulting depression can be built and broadened.

OUR STRENGTHS AND HUMAN RESILIENCIES IN CHALLENGING DESTINY

The human spirit is the one of the most resilient and amazing phenomena of our fragile existence. Time and again, under the most horrific circumstances, evidence shows that individuals can survive and even thrive. In the lifetime of every person some incident or trial will test the core strength of that person's being. The level of the stress that the specific trial may bring is relative. For example, a divorce is always stressful and involves upheaval, even in the best of circumstances. How the parties involved manage the stress can be dependent upon the resiliency of the individual. Early childhood neglect and abuse create a foundation for the individual upon which all other stressors fall. The more resilient the person, the greater her adaptive functioning will be in the world when other negative life stressors befall her. Divorce, major illness, physical illness, tragic accidents, loss of a loved one, job loss, war, and a myriad of other tragedies can befall the adult. When these issues are compounded by the early vulnerabilities of abuse, neglect, or tragedy, the effects can potentially be catastrophic if the individual is not resilient.

George Bonanno described resiliency as a dynamic process of healthy adaptation in the face of severe adversity. The resiliency of the human spirit has been seen in even the most soul-destroying circumstances. The world has been witness to individuals who have somehow survived the Holocaust, the bombings of Hiroshima and Nagasaki, world wars, and extreme personal suffering and poverty. Not only have these individuals survived unbelievable trauma, but many have gone on to lead productive lives that have had a positive impact on others and on society. How is it possible for some to have the emotional and spiritual capacity to recover enough from tragedy to function effectively in life? Why do others fall into despair and lose all hope?

Jon Shaw reports that during childhood, even when the environment is not optimal for the development of a healthy self, some internal resiliencies may be the result of unknown genetic determinants. Genetic resiliency factors are internal biological and personality characteristics with which the infant is born that can facilitate some individuals in moving forward and prospering even when they have faced what can appear to be insurmountable odds.

These inherent genetic traits that can fortify a sense of hope even in extraordinarily bleak conditions are mysterious and as yet undefined by research. Remarkably, some infants who are born into miserable circumstances have an intrinsically better ability to thrive than others born into the same set of circumstances. Genetic resiliency is an area in which information is sparse. Research into the neuropsychological pathways of the infant are needed. Further information could provide a wealth of understanding in explaining how some infants intrinsically are born better fortified to withstand trauma than are other newborns.

While the genetic origins of resiliency may be mysterious, the environmental factors that contribute to surviving and thriving are much clearer. These elements are generally referred to as *protective factors* and can result in child and adult adaptive behaviors under adverse circumstances.

There are many environmental protective factors that can help an individual to be resilient. Diane Papalia, Sally Wendos Olds, and Ruth Feldman describe having a supportive environment as one of the most important elements in developing resiliency. As previously discussed, many of the early vulnerability factors for suicide are the result of children living in homes where there is not a safe or consistent environment provided by their caregivers. If a child is raised by caregivers who are attuned and attentive, internal resiliency will be built as mental health issues or suicidal tendencies are managed in a loving and caring manner. However, the child or infant who is raised by unaware or abusive caregivers begins life at an extraordinary disadvantage. A powerful protective factor for this disadvantaged infant or child would be to have at least one other person in his environment with whom he can feel safe, esteemed, or hopeful. This "important other" could be a distant relative, a teacher, a grandparent, or a neighbor. Even when contact with a caring adult may be limited and appear to be superficial, the meaning that the child can make from a positive interaction with one adult can have a profoundly reparative effect on an abused or neglected child. The relationship that a child can have with an important other can foster some of the positive experiences that the child may be lacking in the home environment. Words of praise from a teacher, a kind gesture from an extended family member, an invitation to a neighbor's dinner table, and words of support can increase a child's positive sense of self. According to Katey Baruth and Jane Carroll, the important others in a child's life become even more crucial when the child is not experiencing positive interactions at home. Resilient individuals are likely to have a family member, friend, or encouraging community member who provides a trusted and supportive environment or relationship.

Additionally, a child's perception of a supportive other can also provide positive effects. For example, a teacher may have kind words for all members of a class, but the vulnerable child may perceive that the words from the teacher are meant for him alone. Results from a study by Jeremiah Schumm, Melissa Phillips, and Stevan Hobfoll on interpersonal trauma and resiliency suggest that social support may buffer the cumulative effect of child and adult interpersonal trauma and that perceived social support serves a buffering role for survivors of child abuse and adult rape. Interactions with a positive adult role model can clearly help to provide a sense of hope for youngsters, even if the contact with the important other is limited. A child may have access to a kind and supportive grandparent only once or twice a year; however, this support may be meaningful enough to help the child feel a sense of being loved and esteemed by someone in the world. These positive feelings can help to improve self-esteem and self-efficacy, and promote overall well-being in the child. The impact of the positive important other in the life of an abused or neglected child cannot be minimized. In fact, little kindnesses that others can provide in the early years help to foster hope and resilience and improve the individual's ability to combat despair and suicidal tendencies throughout the life span.

Diane Papalia states that along with having an important other to help foster resiliency, the impact of having compensating experiences can be instrumental in fortifying strength and survival in the child and in later years in the adult. Compensating experiences are events in which the child or adult is able to achieve attainable goals. These goals may be clearly set markers or may be naturally developing mastery over life's transitional events. For example, the very young child will feel pleasure when she is able to grasp and hold an object that has previously been out of her ability to hold. The older child will feel a sense of accomplishment as she becomes successful in mastering her environment and play. For a developing child, building a tower of blocks or learning to tie her shoes can be a matter of great self-pride. Additionally, when a child is able to complete a task successfully, this is a marker to her that she is competent. This feeling of mastery is based on what is visible and concrete; even if the child does not receive positive feedback from the caregiver, she bears witness to her own success. These compensating experiences can begin in early childhood and continue as the child successfully completes the developmental stages of growth. As the compensating experiences grow, so does the child's knowledge that she is bright, competent, and successful. The child's self-esteem improves from her own positive outcomes, and resiliency to outside forces develops and strengthens.

Even for adults, compensating experiences can be especially helpful in building and maintaining resiliency. If an adult has repeated failures in one area of his life but also has reparative, successful experiences in another area, he will be more likely to retain a positive sense of self. This positive sense of well-being, in turn, fosters resiliency and a better ability to manage the effects of failure.

Positive experiences with friendship are also experiences that can help both children and adults to feel an improved sense of self. Friendships help the child to build an internal understanding that she can have fulfilling relationships. These early peer relationships can be crucial factors in compensating for limited positive responses from the child's caretaker. A child who does not receive attention or positive response at home but who develops early friendships may be able to internalize important experiences of love from her companions. While her home life may be barren of much-needed affection, seeds of warmth can be garnished from the environment through friendships that may create hope and fill the empty soul. Both in childhood and in later adulthood, friends can take on the role of important others and may be a great source of support. As the child or adult feels esteem through the eyes of a friend, this positive regard helps the vulnerable individual to flourish. Friendships foster resiliency and decrease depression and isolation. Friendships are a protective factor against depression and subsequent completed suicide.

Diane Papalia and others describe another protective factor as having an adaptable personality. The infant or child with an adaptable temperament is more likely to be resilient under adverse circumstances. An infant is born with any number of characteristics that are unique to him, which make up his unique and individual temperament. These traits, which are present at birth, are hard-wired in the infant's brain and help to organize the child's approach to the world. Because of this wiring, some infants may have the innate ability to withstand a neglectful environment with greater positive outcome than other infants experiencing the same kind of negative early experience. Research clearly inform us of how the child's genetics, culture, and environment play a part in how the child responds to its world. The formation of innate temperament traits, however, may be some of the more mysterious components in the development of the infant. As with genetics, further research is needed to address the differences in temperament that accompany the infant into the world.

Some infants are born with irritable, finicky, nervous, and distressed characteristics that make up their temperament. The infant with these personality characteristics is more vulnerable to continued difficulties in later life. Unfortunately, these infants and children are more susceptible to increased abuse or neglect because their personalities require more sustained attention from their caretakers. As the infant with a distressed temperament whines and cries out its unknown frustrations, the caregiver can become exhausted and overwhelmed and may be unable to be attentive in a positive manner. This finicky infant may then have further difficulty adapting to the inconsistencies of the challenged caregiver, which can, in turn, result in an increase in the child's needs. A negative cycle can be created between child and parent, and abuse or neglect may heighten in response to the demands of the child. The little person who is born with distressed characteristics enters the world at a disadvantage. Ultimately, this infant can be more vulnerable to disrupted early relationships that may impact later adult functioning and lead to subsequent depression and suicidal predisposition.

Conversely, the infant born with an adaptable temperament is more equipped to survive and grow even in a less than optimal environment. This small person seems to have the innate capacity to minimize the internal impact of negative experiences and, in a manner of speaking, roll with the punches. This infant is born into the world with the ability to survive chaos and unpredictability more easily than the previously described nervous infant. The adaptable infant and child greet the world with less intensity and distractibility, less irritability, greater mood stability, and a core of persistence. This infant is less likely to draw the wrath of the caregiver and, thus, may minimize the effects of abuse. With an adaptable personality, an infant draws others to him like moths to a flame. He coos and gurgles and entertains adults with his easy style. When there are parenting failures, this infant appears to be less apt to suffer the consequences.

As stated, birth temperament is somewhat mysterious. The infant's temperament may not be tied at all to the parenting or birth environment of the child. At times, it appears to be a random phenomenon whether a child is born with a distressed, finicky personality or with an easy, affable personality. The consequences of birth temperament, however, can be life altering.

A child who is born with an adaptable nature fosters and builds resilience throughout the life span. The person who is adaptable and has the ability to experience trauma without becoming overwhelmed by it will have improved functioning in all his daily routines and life events. This ability to be adaptable can help an individual to move through the kind of depression and hopelessness that can lead to suicidal tendencies. Although the adaptable person may still be faced with trauma, stress, and feelings of despair, he will be more resilient in the management of life's inevitable turmoil.

Papalia and others note as a final protective factor that the infant who is born into an environment with fewer stressors is more resilient than the infant who is born into a home of chaos and upheaval. Furthermore, individuals throughout the life span appear to be less vulnerable to depression and subsequent suicide when life stressors are kept to a minimum. Michelle Dumont and Marc Provost's research has shown that "resilient persons" are likely to have experienced fewer life stressors and risk factors when compared to less resilient individuals. Common sense dictates that a person who goes through life with few challenges may have an easier time of surviving and thriving than another person who may have many life obstacles to surmount. A child who has enough to eat, warm clothing, parental affection and consistency, and the opportunity for an education will not have the same hurdles to master as the underprivileged child faces. The growing individual with less internal and environmental stress will develop a sturdy sense of self, which is a strong protective factor against suicidal predisposition.

Protective factors also may be cultural in nature. Cultural identification can increase a sense of belonging, social support, and adaptive functioning. Phillip Bowman said, "Cultural strengths facilitate adaptive coping and, in turn, well-being and health; and multilevel cultural strengths promote role resiliency by reducing risky cognitive analyses such as role discouragement, self-blame and hopelessness." Bowman goes on to state that "protective cultural strengths help to explain why some at-risk youth maintain a sense of hope, vitality, and persistence and excel against discouraging odds. Cultural strengths may reduce feelings of being overwhelmed, cut off, or dispirited." Religious and spiritual affiliations can also provide the individual with a sense of meaning and belonging. For a vulnerable youngster, the connection to a community church can not only provide an escape from home but also may instill meaning and hope to an existence that could otherwise feel emotionally barren.

As noted, there are numerous protective factors that can serve to buffer the individual's vulnerabilities to suicidal tendencies. Environmental, adaptive, social, religious, and cultural factors can help the child who is living in an environment that is abusive or neglectful to develop and build resiliencies that can help her to function in the world. Many children do survive and master vulnerabilities when one or more protective factors are in place. The child may have an important other who helps to build her sense of self, she may have a strong sense of culture or ethnicity that gives her purpose, or she may have an adaptable personality that helps her to minimize the negative impact of her environment. Each protective factor acts as a shield against hopelessness and despair, which can lead to suicidal thought. Protective factors build resiliency for the current obstacles the child may face in life and for the events to come.

Interestingly, the strength and resiliency of an individual is often seen most clearly in the wake of a personal tragedy or loss. Once an individual experiences a tragic event and is able to cope with the aftermath of the event and the accompanying feelings, he may then experience a sense of mastery and a knowledge that he can survive. This can be a powerful realization and bring with it a feeling of hope that he will be able to cope with any further life travails. Self-efficacy and optimism are both important elements in resilience. According to Karen Reivich and Andrew Shatte, hope is a crucial element in combating despair, and when an individual is able to survive and master a traumatic event, his ability to hope can be fortified. The fortification of an individual's hope further strengthens his resilience for the challenges that life will certainly present.

Specific Protective Factors That Can Reduce Adult Suicidality:

- Having an "important, caring other"
- Consistent, loving environment
- Genetic resiliency
- Adaptive personality
- Feelings of mastery (doing well in play and at school)
- Friendships
- Religious affiliation
- Social support
- Cultural identification
- An environment with limited stress
- Hope

Building and fortifying an individual's resiliencies can begin to be developed at an early age or can develop over time. External and internal mechanisms can be utilized to build resiliency in vulnerable individuals. If the seeds for resiliency can be planted early in the life of the individual, then it is less likely that this person will develop suicidal tendencies in later life. However, even in later life, resiliencies can be built that may be just as powerful in thwarting depression and subsequent suicidal thought or action.

EXTERNALLY BUILT RESILIENCY

External mechanisms for building hope, strength, and adaptability in children can come from the important others or the community. The earlier the intervention occurs, the greater the positive impact will be on the child. Often, the adult who has great influence on a child and who is an important other does not have a clear understanding that he or she is fulfilling such a crucial role. Therefore, to increase the resiliency that develops within the child from the intervention of an external source, an awareness of the impact of these forces must be increased. For example, the teacher who has a kind word for a quiet child may not realize just how crucial these words can be; the loving grandparent might not understand that comforting words can make all the difference in the world of a small child. Some children have the first consistent and nurturing experience in their lives in church, after-school programs, sports, or other school-sponsored activities. Oftentimes these vulnerable children attempt to escape their dysfunctional home circumstances by spending as much time as possible at school. The wise educator understands that these children need more from them than formal education; they need encouragement and words of support. What may seem to be small inconsequential kindnesses in some circumstances can have a monumental impact on a developing self that is hungry for attention and praise. The school is a place that a child can experience positive reparative interactions with adults and begin to hear alternative perspectives than what she is exposed to in the home.

Church, a community recreation program, or another sponsored program may also be places in the world of a vulnerable child that can have a significant positive impact. A camp counselor who reaches out and spends a few extra moments with a quiet child may begin to show this child that he is lovable and worthy of attention. A spiritual leader or church member who helps redirect a child who is acting out to a new set of behaviors may unknowingly be one of the only adults who has taken this initiative with the youngster.

Providing positive attention to children may seem to make simple common sense; unfortunately, this is not always the way that youngsters are treated in the world. Some educators and community leaders may be overwhelmed by the level of need they see in these children and may not have the skills or resources to manage the emotional issues that these special young people bring to the classroom and community. There are times when youth can be further victimized in the community as their behaviors are misunderstood as inattention or rebellion.

Training programs in the schools and community are often available to help providers recognize and assist children who are vulnerable and at risk for depression and hopelessness. These training programs are valuable reminders for providers of how a simple action by an external resource can make a significant difference in a child's life and subsequent development. Ongoing, free caregiver classes may also be provided in communities to address the basics of raising a healthy and happy child. Local workshops for the general public that review the basics of listening and providing feedback to children are useful for anyone who provides care to children. These workshops may be offered in a church, library, or school; listings for the topic, time, and date of these workshops may be found in the local newspaper or online. Some of the information that is provided at these workshops and trainings may seem simple; however, the act of attending and being reminded that the use of basic strategies to assist children grow into healthy adults can be crucial. The community workshops that teach such topics as promoting self-esteem in children or listening skills also provide an opportunity for adults to network and build their own support systems. These networks can be a wonderful resource for other opportunities that may be available in the community. Supportive relationships may be formed by those in attendance, and word-of-mouth referrals to other training programs propel the continuum of good care for our children.

When the primary caregivers are not available to provide a consistent and loving home environment for their children, it becomes the responsibility of every other adult in that child's life to step forward. Even if it is only for a moment, any small positive intervention can have a lasting impact on the child. When positive external resources are present for the child either in the home, school, church, or community, resiliency strategies are imparted to a child for managing distress. As these external resources expand to multiple sources that provide positive feedback to the child, the early risk factors that can ultimately lead to suicidal tendencies may be mitigated.

INTERNALLY BUILT RESILIENCY

Internal mechanisms for developing resiliencies come from within, although seeds may be planted from an external source(s). These internal mechanisms are either personality based or develop over time as the child grows into an adult. Some internal elements of resilience include developing strong coping skills, having a sense of humor, setting and achieving goals, changing automatic negative thoughts, developing purpose and meaning in life, and having hope. The foundation for the development of such positive internal resources may be imparted by an important other or learned by the adaptable child.

Internal coping skills include many strategies that can be crucial for the individual's emotional and physical survival in an abusive world. For the young child, coping with an unpredictable life may mean developing skills that provide physical safety. At a very early age children can gain the understanding that they need to remain quiet or in their room when the caregivers are intoxicated or raging. This withdrawal to safety is considered to be a coping skill and may come from an internal sense of survival. The child that learns to put herself out of harm's way and to stay safe is positively reinforced by avoiding the pain of a beating or verbal abuse. The positive reinforcement leads to a continuation of the behavior of withdrawal and, thus, to further safety. While withdrawal may not be a functional adult coping mechanism, in an abusive child's life it is a very good strategy. As the child grows, her coping skills may develop to include staying later at school or spending as much time at a friend's home as possible.

Another learned and developed coping skill is presenting a compliant self to the world. While many children in abusive or neglectful homes feel anger and sadness, they learn to hide these feelings and show the world a false happy face. In this way, they may keep the parent satisfied and further keep themselves from the potential wrath of their caregiver. Children in abusive and neglectful homes tend to be hypervigilant and generally are very aware of the mood of their caretaker. If they detect that their parent is in an abusive mood, they will adapt their personality to a mood that they may not be feeling to please and soothe the caretaker. Once again, while in adulthood compliance is not necessarily a functional trait, the child in an unpredictable home uses this strategy to remain safe.

Children in unsafe environments may also adapt themselves to becoming the home caretaker. They may need to care for and protect younger siblings and keep them quiet when they perceive the adult is drunk or apt to be abusive. They may need to take on the role of the adult by getting themselves and their brothers and sisters up for school, making sure there is something to eat, and keeping the home clean. This role of parentified child is another functional coping skill for children in abusive environments. As they master the skills needed to keep daily routines and to stay fed, clean, and safe, they build internal resiliency. They master an unsafe environment.

Some children cope and, oddly enough, build internal resiliency by living in a fantasy world. These children may bury themselves in books, music, television, and other electronic devices such as DVDs and MP3s. Their fantasy lives provide them with distance from their painful real worlds and also can provide them with hope that life can be different. As these children view the media version of how other families live their lives on television, they may come to believe that life can be different. Their immersion in fantasy may help to keep them partially protected from the harsh reality that may be their world.

Although these coping skills may not be thought of as positive resources, for the child these skills are functional and help to keep her safe in her unsafe world. Indeed, not only do these strategies keep the child out of harm's way, they also can provide an additional inner strength as she learns that there is hope, that she can master her environment even when it is dangerous, and that she can survive treacherous circumstances. The knowledge that she can manage her life in a harrowing environment creates an internal resiliency and the knowledge that she can survive.

As these youngsters grow into adulthood, some of these early coping strategies will no longer be functional. The coping patterns for survival that were developed by these young minds and that helped to build internal resiliency in childhood will no longer be viewed as positive internal resources. In fact, some of the strategies that these young people used and mastered to keep safe will impact them in adulthood in negative ways. For example, living in a fantasy world or being compliant as an adult may not help an adult individual to flourish, and, in fact, could have a negative impact on an adult's life. These adults will need to learn new and more effective methods of managing adversity. Unfortunately, some early patterns of development are challenging to change, and it may require the help of a counselor to design new and healthier life patterns.

Another important internal resource for any child is both cognitive and emotional intelligence. A bright child will quickly learn patterns that can keep her from harm and may be less likely to repeat behaviors that will cause her to be threatened by the caregiver. When a child is bright, she will easily pick up nuances from the adults in her world. The ability to grasp what the caregiver expects from her and the cognitive knowledge to respond appropriately helps the child to receive positive energy from her parent. Intelligence that results from a high IQ leads to cognitive strengths; the child will have a stronger chance of understanding what she needs to do and have the ability to then respond in a fashion that reaps her rewards. These children will quickly learn to mimic the behaviors that get them the desired response.

Children with good emotional intelligence also may fare better in their environment. These children understand with a high degree of complexity the emotional world around them and respond accordingly. The child who is emotionally bright will pick up on a parent's sadness or internal emotional state and match his own personality in response. This is not the same strategy the hypervigilant child uses when afraid and who then becomes compliant or withdrawn; rather, this is a child who comprehends the emotional state of his world and reacts accordingly. The result of being a child with a higher state of emotional intelligence is that the adults surrounding him may feel understood and, thus, drawn in a positive way to the child.

Having a higher cognitive or emotional intelligence can also promote a child's sense of humor. Humor is generally found in children who are bright, and humor can be a protective factor as it keeps the individual's spirits up even in adverse circumstances. The child who is able to laugh and find amusement in her world will move through life more easily than one who is unable to use this cognitive strength. As the child matures, humor can also lead the young person to understand paradox in adversity, and this understanding can be a protective factor against otherwise bleak circumstances. Humor is an internal resource that builds resiliency. Additionally, when a child has a sense of humor, she tends to be better liked by others in her environment, and this likability can provide a secondary advantage of safety.

Finally, hope is an internal resource that builds resiliency. The ability to have hope that there will be an eventual positive outcome is essential to ensure emotional well-being. If hope does not exist, despair and despondency can form and solidify a toxic inner world. The ability to hope that life will be different and to believe that painful circumstances can change can make any current conflict more manageable. Hope is the antidote to hopelessness. Hope may be an elusive concept to a child caught in a family cycle of violence and chaos, but for those children who are able to find and hold on to hope, the ability to withstand their family dysfunction and be resilient is magnified.

How does hope develop and grow in some and diminish in others? The presence of at least one of the protective factors that have been discussed may lead a child to find a seed of hope and cling to it. This seed of hope can be cultivated as the child moves into the outer world and sees that not all families or circumstances are bleak and that there is potential for kindness and positive response from others in the world. Hope can also flourish as the child sees the world through the media; while the media may not project a real-life image of how all families act, it still may offer alternatives to the belief that all homes are abusive.

Positive expectations, or hope, closely relates to the concept of self-efficacy. Self-efficacy refers to the expectation that one's behavior will be effective. When someone believes that he can have an impact on his environment, this hope leads to action; therefore, feelings of helplessness decrease. Children who can hope are more apt to successfully combat depression and subsequent suicidal tendencies. They are able to believe that their lives will improve; they trust that somehow the abuser will stop the abuse, that they will be loved, or that someone will rescue them. The internal ability to hope fosters the desire to survive. Hope is a powerful friend to building and maintaining resiliency and a crucial antidote to despair.

The following chapter will detail specific methods of recovery and coping strategies for the suicidal person. For those individuals who have some internal and external resiliency factors already in place, the recovery process may be easier. However, resiliency factors can be developed and learned at any stage of the life span, even when vulnerabilities are great. Chapter 4 spells out a specific common sense plan for recovery from depression and suicidal intent.

Her mother was an alcoholic, and by the time Julia was five, she had become the caretaker in the family. She would look after her little brother,
make sure that he was fed and changed, and even try to make her mother
eat and go to bed. At age five Julia had been very bright and cute. She had
known how to stay out of her mother's way when her moods would shift.
Julia would take her brother with her to play games in another room, away
from their mother's potential anger, which could harm them. She could
remember being afraid that she might not be able to feed her brother because there was not enough food in the cabinet. Sometimes they ate only
cereal, and many times there was nothing to drink but water. Julia could
not recall her father. For many years Julia had thought that her family was
like everyone else's family.

Her mother had many boyfriends. They were generally nice to Julia
and her brother in the beginning; then it seemed that they would lose
interest in them. At first, Julia had thought that one of the boyfriends
might marry their mother and it would be like a Disney movie; they would
be taken care of and loved. But after many men had passed in and out of
the apartment, Julia figured out that these men just didn't care about her.
Once, when her mother was passed out in the living room, one of the men
had come into the room that Julia shared with her brother. The man told
her to be quiet and not to tell when he touched her. He came into her
room many times, and Julia knew that her mother would not stop him.
This man had stayed with her mother longer than the others, and he had
made sure that they had food and got to school on time. There were many
loud fights between her mother and the man at night, and Julia knew that
after a fight the man would come to her room. She had never liked to use
his name and still thought of him as "the man." These were the years that
Julia began to feel like she was in a dark room that she could not escape.

Julia's brother would come home much later than her after school on
the bus, so every day Julia had time to herself to visit her neighbor, Miss
Harper, who lived on the first floor. She would wait there and watch out
the window for her brother's bus to arrive. Julia loved to go to Miss Harper's apartment. Miss Harper would always have a snack ready for her, and
she would sit on her couch and listen to Miss Harper's stories. Julia would
cozy up on the couch, and sometimes Miss Harper would put her arm
around Julia or cover her with a warm blanket. Julia's memories of Miss
Harper were the best ones she could remember. Julia wished she lived with
Miss Harper all the time. She would sometimes watch from the window in
her own upstairs apartment and would see when Miss Harper went out to
shop or do errands. When Julia got older, she would help Miss Harper
shovel the walkway and sometimes make snacks to eat. They would watch

the same soap opera on television together every day, and Julia smiled when she thought that she still liked to watch that program sometimes.

It seemed to Julia, in looking back, that once she had realized that there were people and families in the world who could show affection and kindness like Miss Harper, she had had a harder time wanting to wake up. The dark room had become darker. She could remember consciously thinking at a young age that she wished she would just go to sleep and right to heaven.

Julia could clearly remember the first time she had decided that she wanted to die. She had been 14. The sexual abuse had stopped when she was 11; the man just never came back one day. Her mother's drinking seemed to be the same; she would pass out on the couch, and it was really like Julia was the mother. Julia thought she could make sure her brother would be taken care of if she died by writing a letter to her uncle who lived in California. Julia wrote the letter and mailed it. Julia had not been quite sure how to die, but she thought that if she took all her mother's pills, she would go to sleep and not wake up. Julia thought her mother would never know if she didn't wake up, and there would be enough time for Julia to go to sleep forever. The day that Julia had mailed the letter to her uncle she took a full bottle of medication that was in her mother's cabinet. She remembered that she had felt very calm and settled with her decision.

Instead of falling asleep, Julia became very, very ill. She experienced extraordinary stomach cramping, and the pain was so bad that she went for help to Miss Harper, who called an ambulance. Julia's mother was not at home.

Julia remembered that this was the first of several suicide attempts that she made between the time she was age 14 and age 22. She had been hospitalized twice for her attempts. Once, Julia had cut her wrists so deeply that she still wore longer sleeves when she wanted to hide the scars. She had been assigned a counselor, but Julia had learned not to tell her family secrets, so the counselor had not really understood. Julia had liked going to counseling because she had felt safe there, but she had not shared her deep pain or the level of depression she was feeling. When Julia was 18, she had her first boyfriend, and she fell in love with him. This had been the most important relationship Julia had ever known. When he broke up with her, she was devastated and had known she had a final choice. She was either going to kill herself or try to do something to stop the negative thought patterns that seemed to be poisoning her mind.

For the first time, Julia had sought help from a counselor herself. The counselor was a warm woman who had wanted Julia to call her Ginny. Ginny was very skilled in understanding and working with the kind of pain a young woman like Julia was carrying inside her. Julia slowly had opened up to Ginny about her past. Ginny assessed Julia and determined that Julia was most likely suffering from a depression that was both biological in nature and exaggerated by environmental factors. Although Julia had been diagnosed with depression when she was younger, she had not understood or cared what that meant. This time, Julia had wanted to see if she could stop the suicidal thoughts and feel better about herself and her life. Ginny referred Julia to a psychiatric nurse practitioner, who could provide Julia with the correct medication to decrease her depression. Julia began to sleep better at night. She found that her appetite improved and that she was able to stop some of the negative thoughts with the skills that Ginny taught her. When she had felt suicidal, or if the negative thoughts returned, Julia learned to use self-soothing techniques to fill up the empty space inside her. She and Ginny had an agreement that if Julia felt she was going to harm herself, she would call either Ginny or the Suicide Help Line. Over time, Ginny helped Julia to see that she was a good and lovable person. Julia experienced moments of great sadness and loss in her therapy regarding her childhood, but she also recalled Miss Harper and how comforted she had felt by this kind woman. Julia began to take the memories of the warmth from Miss Harper and use these memories when she needed to feel loved. She also began to build present-day supports in her life with others who were equally as loving and available.

Today, Julia knew when she was having a bad day. She recognized the signs of her depression, and she knew what she needed to do for herself. She called her new therapist, someone she needed to see only now and then. She set up an appointment and realized that she might need to go back on medication for a period of time. Julia had learned that once the symptoms of depression began, she needed to take action before she became suicidal. Julia was very familiar with the emotional triggers that could lead to her depression, such as the darker winter months or stress. She did not want to return to the dark room. She knew she needed to call for help.

THERE IS HOPE

Suicidal predisposition is not a fatal diagnosis for completed suicide. Many individuals with suicidal thoughts and behaviors are able to recover and move on to lead healthy, adaptive lives. Understanding and intervention can alter negative life experiences that may lead some individuals who are born and raised with suicidal vulnerabilities to recovery. Depression is a very treatable illness with an excellent recovery rate when help is obtained.

Each individual's experience and recovery is different from everyone else's experience and recovery. There is no specific map for recovery; each person is unique and has a unique set of experiences; therefore, each recovery plan will need to be adapted to the individual's own needs and life history.

Some individuals reach out for help at the first suicidal thought. They may feel frightened by the images of their own death and have an instinct of self-preservation that propels them to reach out for assistance. Asking for help and telling someone about suicidal thoughts is an important step in the recovery process.

The people who develop support systems can use these resources when the feelings of self-harm become overwhelming. Once a professional is included in the support network, the suicidal individual will also have clinical resources that can further decrease suicidal intent. The professional will assist the suicidal person in developing a safety plan and fortifying a support network to use when needed. Cognitive interventions and medication may be suggested by the professional to reduce suicidality. Clinical research indicates that the reduction of suicidal symptoms is dramatic in depressed individuals who receive both psychotherapy and medication.

Some individuals with depression may have experienced suicidal images for many years, never telling anyone. Eventually, these individuals' suicidal thoughts may escalate to suicidal gestures and planned intent for self-harm. Important others surrounding these suicidal people may not be aware of the distress these individuals are experiencing and may be deeply surprised when a suicide attempt is made. Although there are generally signs that a person is experiencing depression, these signs may be subtle and not easily recognized or understood to be serious. Depression is sometimes referred to as a "silent killer" because it can be so lethal, and the symptoms of hopelessness and withdrawal may not be seen by others.

Once depression is identified and suicidal thoughts are uncovered, it is crucial that supports be put in place. The supports that can lead to recovery may vary, depending on the circumstances and wishes of the person. Recognizing suicidal tendencies, external resources, strategies, and coping skills that can be helpful to the suicidal individual will be described in detail in the next several pages.

RECOGNIZING SUICIDAL TENDENCIES: WHEN YOU NEED HELP

Depression can begin slowly and be experienced as low-grade lethargy over a long period of time, or it can emerge quickly following a traumatic event or even out of the blue. It is a phenomenon that can be observable to others, or it can be hidden by the individual experiencing the pain. There are signs and symptoms to be aware of for anyone who thinks she may be experiencing depression. Untreated depression can lead to suicidal thought and potentially to self-harm and even completed suicide. Although depression is not always progressive when it is untreated, there remains some risk that it will progress. With treatment depression has an extremely high rate for a successful recovery to full functioning. Therefore, it is important to know the signs of depression and to use the resources noted in this chapter if the symptoms that are described fit what is being experienced.

One of the common symptoms of depression is feeling hopeless. Feelings of hopelessness can be described as not believing that anything good will happen or that life has positive experiences in store in the future. Hopelessness can be a pervasive feeling that affects relationships, work, friendships, and the desire to engage in activities. The person feeling hopeless may ask himself, "What's the point?" This person may lose interest in all the activities that he once enjoyed and begin to isolate himself from friends and family. Feelings of hopelessness can impact all levels of the individual's ability to function, as well as important relationships. It can feel to the hopeless person that life is just not worth living.

Another common symptom of depression is a significant change in sleep patterns and eating habits. The depressed person may find herself sleeping too much or not being able to fall asleep or stay asleep. Oftentimes depressed people find that their thoughts may become cyclic at night when they lie down to go to sleep; simple thoughts may circle around and around in the mind and may lead to other endless thoughts. The harder that this person tries to fall asleep, the more crowded her mind becomes with thoughts. Nighttime can become torturous as she finds herself tossing until the wee hours of the morning. These folks with disrupted sleep must then face the next day already at a disadvantage. They are overtired and still fighting depression. Conversely, others with sleep disruption related to depression may find that they are sleeping endless hours and are having difficulty getting out of bed. They may find that all they want to do is sleep and then still not feel rested when they are awake. If someone is either not able to sleep or finds herself sleeping all the time, her daily functioning will be interrupted. This can contribute to the onset of a depressive episode or increase already present depression.

A significant change in eating habits can also be a sign of the onset of depression. Some individuals may experience a dramatic weight loss over a short period of time as they lose their appetite and interest in food. The taste of food can become bland, and the idea of preparing a meal or even of summoning the energy to eat can seem to be too much. Others may misinterpret the weight loss as a good thing in this culture in which being thinner is often rewarded. The person who is losing weight rapidly may not understand that his appetite has decreased because he is depressed. Losing a substantial amount of weight in a short period of time is a signal that something is wrong.

Another change in eating that can be a factor in depression may be a significant increase in weight over a short period of time. This can be caused as the depressed person seeks to self-soothe by eating everything in sight. As the weight increases, the depressed person's physical system becomes slowed, and the depression may be compounded by the additional pounds that she is carrying.

The depressed person may lose ambition and the energy to get to work on time or at all. This individual may find himself crying for no reason at all and sometimes have difficulty stopping. His concentration and memory can be impaired, and the smallest tasks may seem to take great energy. Depressed individuals can also find that they are increasing their use of substances to blunt the emotional pain that they are experiencing. Alcohol and most drugs are depressants, and the increased use of substances can further plunge the person into increased depression.

Depression is an illness that can create disruption in many aspects of someone's life. Important relationships can be adversely impacted as the depressed person withdraws from the world. Her spouse or partner and friends may not understand what has happened to the person that they once knew to be lively and energized. Interest in sexual activity generally declines as depression increases, and this can create concern or conflict in a relationship. Usual household chores and involvement with children may decrease and cause further conflict. Those who are closest to the depressed person will be impacted the most, and their reactions can further plunge the individual into inertia.

It can sometimes be difficult for the depressed person to recognize and/ or admit to himself or others that he may be depressed. Depression is a mental illness that may not be accepted by some, so an individual may try to "pull themselves up by their bootstraps" as they might have been taught to do in childhood. Unfortunately, this does not necessarily work because depression is often biologically based and may require medical intervention with medication. As much as one may try, sheer willpower may not cure this illness. If someone is experiencing the symptoms noted above the best thing to do is to talk to a professional. *Depression is treatable. There is hope.*

There are times when it is imperative for the depressed person to recognize her symptoms and *get help immediately*. The following symptoms can be warning precursors to suicidal action. Symptoms that require immediate attention include having thoughts about taking one's own life, planning how death can be attempted, giving away belongings, feeling as if death is the only way to solve a problem(s), talking or writing about committing suicide, having the means to commit suicide (weapons, pills), and feeling a need to make out a will or plan one's own funeral. Asking for help may seem to be a daunting task for the depressed person, but it is exactly what she needs to do as soon as she becomes aware that she is experiencing any of these signs of serious mood decline.

Symptoms of Depression:

- Hopelessness
- Sleep disruption
- Significant weight gain or loss
- Loss of energy
- Increased substance use
- Impaired concentration and memory
- Crying bouts
- Self-destructive thoughts
- Poor sense of self
- Negative thinking
- Isolation
- Moodiness
- Always feeling run down

Symptoms of Depression That Are Increased in Severity:

- Giving away possessions and favorite objects
- Talking about death and dying
- Feeling suicidal
- Preoccupation with wills and insurance
- Becoming unusually violent or taking dangerous risks
- Talking or writing about suicide

Symptoms of Depression That Require Immediate Intervention:

- When someone states that he or she is going to commit suicide
- When someone has a plan of how he or she will commit suicide

- When someone has suicidal thoughts and access to the means to commit suicide (weapons, drugs)

STRATEGIES FOR THE SUICIDAL PERSON

The single most important strategy for the suicidal person in her recovery
is to recognize her feelings and to talk about them with a trusted other.
The suicidal person may be experiencing feelings of hopelessness and hold
the belief that nothing will help; thus, reaching out can require tremen-
dous effort. This effort to reach out may be the first and one of the most
crucial steps in her recovery. Once the suicidal individual has disclosed
her feelings, she will no longer be alone with her distress. If she has chosen to talk to a family member or friend, this trusted person can assist her
in reaching out to a mental health professional. If the suicidal person has
directly called a suicide hotline or counselor, the professional will work to
get her connected to resources that can facilitate her healing.

It is important that the suicidal person knows that there is help and
that depression is a treatable illness. Specific thoughts, feelings, and behaviors indicate that someone should get help right away. These may include the wish to die, thinking about ways to die and making a plan,
giving away possessions, believing that death is the only way to solve
problems, losing interest in usual activities, and engaging in risky behaviors. If someone is experiencing these issues, he should reach out immediately to a family member, a friend, or one of the community resources
noted above and at the end of this chapter. At times, suicidal individuals
may feel that suicidal thought is a sign of weakness and that they should
be able to handle their problems on their own. It is important to know
that suicidal thought is usually a symptom of depression and not anyone's
fault; it does not have to be dealt with alone and, in fact, is best managed
with a professional. The suicidal person should know that counseling and
medicine can help. In fact, the prognosis for depression and for people
with suicidal thought is excellent when treated with both therapy and
medication. With treatment, the symptoms of depression that include suicidality can disappear. There is hope.

The suicidal person may not know what to say when she first speaks
with a concerned other or picks up the telephone to call a counselor.
The best strategy is to use words that are honest to describe feelings and
behaviors. For example, "I have not been feeling like there is any point to
living anymore" or "I don't feel like eating, and all I want to do is sleep"
or "Sometimes I wish I didn't have to wake up." If the suicidal person
is speaking with an untrained friend or family member, he may not

understand the seriousness of the conversation, so it may be necessary for the suicidal person to find someone who truly understands and talk to that person.

If You Are Feeling Suicidal:

- Call a professional (listed under "Counselors" in directories).
- Call the local or national hotline (1-800-273-TALK [8255]) anytime day, night, or weekend.
- Talk to a trusted other (friend, family member, church leader, health care worker). Use clear, direct words such as "I don't feel like living anymore and I think I need help."
- Talk to another trusted person if you do not feel understood the first time you reach out.
- Keep talking until you find someone who listens and understands.
- Know that depression is treatable and recovery rates are quite high.

WHEN SOMEONE YOU ARE CONCERNED ABOUT NEEDS HELP

There are many signs and symptoms that help to identify someone who may be experiencing suicidal thought and feelings. Some of these signs may be easily recognizable, while others are cloaked and often invisible to the observer. Observable signs for concern can include many changes in behavior. One of these behavioral changes could be a disruption in sleep patterns. When an individual is depressed, he may sleep too much because he does not have the will or energy to get out of bed. Sleep patterns that are also affected by depression may include the inability to sleep, trouble falling asleep, and trouble staying asleep. Significant changes in eating routines can also be an observable sign of depression. Some individuals who are depressed simply lose their appetite, and weight loss can occur very quickly and dramatically, or over time. Other people who are depressed may attempt to soothe themselves with food and may eat much more than they have in the past. Significant weight gain or weight loss can be an indicator that something is wrong.

Another observable sign that a loved one may be experiencing depression is being moodier or unhappier than usual. This may show itself in episodes of crying, withdrawal from others and isolating oneself, and irritability. Any major change in mood or difference in personality may be a sign that the individual is experiencing emotional issues that need attention. This is especially true if the mood change is dramatic or continues over a period of time. Everyone has times that they feel unhappy or frustrated; the distinction with someone who is depressed is that these periods of moodiness are not fleeting, and they may be very disruptive to the individual's daily functioning or to those around them.

Individuals experiencing depression may appear to be run down and lacking the energy to do the things that they once enjoyed. Usual activities that may have once brought pleasure and interest no longer have any appeal to the depressed person. This individual may isolate and appear withdrawn and tired. Hobbies, physical activity, sexual interest, and other once enjoyable pastimes require more energy than the depressed person can muster.

An increase in the use of substances can also be an observable sign that someone is depressed. Self-medication with chemicals, including alcohol and drugs, may initially help the depressed person mask feelings of sadness and hopelessness. Paradoxically, many of these substances are also depressants and can eventually further plunge the person into a major depression. Compounding this, substance use also can distort thinking and increase impulsivity that can lead to an act of self-harm. Depression and the use of substances can be a lethal combination.

Other observable signs that someone may be depressed or suicidal can be if he begins to give away personal items or if he shows unusual interest in wills, funerals, or insurance policies. If a loved one talks about suicide or wanting to die or states that she doesn't have anything to live for anymore, the concerned person needs to take action. He can encourage his loved one to call a counselor or hotline. If the loved one will not make the call, the concerned person can make the call to the hotline himself to ask what he can do next. It is important that the concerned person does not take on the role of giving advice or trying to solve the other person's problems. These circumstances are best managed by a professional, who can see the situation objectively.

STRATEGIES FOR THE CONCERNED OTHER

The importance of family members and friends cannot be minimized, and this can be especially true when there is a loved one who has suicidal predisposition. Family and friends are the people who are on the front line in the distressed person's battle against depression. They are often the first to observe changes in behaviors and mood, and are often the first to intervene.

When a family member or friend intervenes with a suicidal person, his strategies should include nonjudgmental listening, gentle questions, and facilitating a referral to a professional. There may be some tendency on the part of concerned others to minimize what they are seeing and hearing. Although these minimization impulses may be part of the human defense system and a way to block out the pain of someone who is loved, it is necessary to act on what is heard and not just hope that it will change. Tomorrow the loved one may not feel better, and, in fact, the depression could deepen if untreated. While it is never a concerned person's responsibility if someone completes suicide, he can have some impact to change the outcome.

The first and most important response a concerned other can have with the suicidal person is to take her seriously. It is critical not to judge her or wonder if she is "just seeking attention." If someone makes a suicidal statement, it is, indeed, a cry for help and professional attention is the best intervention to truly determine if there is a possibility of self-harm. Concerned others are not objective and may have difficulty believing that someone they care about is in enough despair to take her own life. While a concerned other may hope that a loved one's mood will change, this is not always the case. If the concerned person does not know what to say or how to intervene with the suicidal individual, she can call the hotline noted above and at the end of this section. The trained hotline staff will coach her in how to best proceed.

If there is ever any threat of imminent harm, the police should be called right away. For example, if someone says, "I have a gun, and I am going to kill myself," it is time to immediately call 911. It is not the role of the concerned person to try to wrestle a weapon away from someone or to hope that the person in despair doesn't really have a gun and is just blowing off steam. The concerned person may have the mistaken assumption that he has the relationship power to convince the family member or friend that she has too much to live for to kill herself. The suicidal person may feel enough pressure from her concerned other in that moment to stop her suicide attempt. However, without professional help the underlying source of the pain will not be dealt with, and the suicidal impulse may resurface. Therefore, when there is any indication that someone has a plan and intent to kill herself, a professional should be called immediately.

It is also important that concerned others do not take on too much sole responsibility for keeping their loved ones safe from self-harm. This can be a monumental task if a person is intent on killing himself and can take a toll on concerned others. If a concerned person finds herself worrying all the time, continually checking to see if the loved one is "okay," or notices the signs and symptoms of depression that are listed in this chapter, she should call a professional counselor or the hotline to talk herself. Dealing with a suicidal person is too much responsibility to carry alone. Caring about others is a wonderful thing, but there are times when this caring should translate into getting a professional involved. The professional is trained both to help the concerned other with her concerns and to coach the concerned person in how to navigate the tumultuous waters that surround a suicidal person.

In less immediate circumstances, if a concerned person is worried about a loved one, there are questions and words to say that can be helpful in guiding the suicidal person to professional help. The concerned person sometimes believes that he can make a person suicidal if he raises the question about suicide. This is not the case. As stated previously, the only person responsible for a completed suicide is the suicidal person herself. Many times the suicidal person will experience a feeling of relief that she is understood and cared about when a concerned other asks questions.

Much like the suicidal person who may not know how to disclose feelings of suicidality, the concerned other may not know how to approach the person she is worried about. The best manner in which to talk to the suicidal person is to be caring and direct. For example, the concerned person could ask, "You have seemed down for a long time, and I've been worried about you. Have you had any thoughts about ending your own life?" Or, the concerned other may ask, "I have been thinking about you, and you don't seem to be yourself. You're sleeping all the time and just don't appear happy. Have you had any thoughts about suicide?"

These questions can be hard for the concerned person to ask but are important for many reasons. If the loved one is indeed suicidal and can admit it, then the journey toward healing has begun. If the loved one is suicidal but is unable to say so, a seed will be planted for her that may later give her permission to go to the concerned other with her feelings. Sometimes the concerned person has to ask more than once if he remains worried and if the signs and symptoms of depression continue. The questions about suicide provide information, create an indication that someone notices and cares, and can begin a process for the individual to get help.

Once the suicidal person is able to disclose that he has had suicidal thoughts, the concerned person can facilitate the helping process. A wonderful follow-up statement to the suicidal person could be, "I can hear that you are really hurting. Let me call this number for you, and after you make an appointment to talk to someone, I would be happy to go with you if you would like." Sometimes the person with suicidal thoughts may not be ready to make an appointment to talk with a professional. This can be very hard for the concerned person, who wants assurance that her loved one will get help. It is good to understand that the first time an appointment is suggested, it is often declined. However, the seed has been planted that there is help available; the hurting person will remember this and may use the resources provided to him at another time. If the person with suicidal thoughts and feelings is unwilling to get help but is not at immediate risk, there is no need to panic or call 911. The concerned person may be worried or upset enough to call the help line herself. She may also decide to seek her own counseling to manage the anxiety she is feeling as a result of fears regarding a loved one's potential self-harm. It is recommended that if someone has concerns regarding another's ability for self-harm that impact her own daily functioning, she should reach out to any of the described resources for her own help. Suicide is a very frightening concept. It needs to be taken seriously, and attention needs to be given, not only to the suicidal individual, but also to concerned persons who are impacted by the potential self-destruction of someone they care about.

If You Are Concerned About Someone Taking Their Own Life:

- Call 911 if you believe threat of suicide is imminent.
- Listen/take your loved one seriously.
- Be nonjudgmental.
- Don't be afraid to ask questions such as, "It seems you have been sad for a long time, and I've been wondering if you've had thoughts about killing yourself?"
- Offer to call a professional or a hotline and offer to accompany your loved one to the first appointment.
- Do not take on too much responsibility or become a "counselor."
- Get help for yourself if you find that you are worrying all the time or have questions about how to help your loved one.
- Call 1-800-273-TALK (8255) for resources and referrals.

USING RESOURCES

External resources for help can be within an arm's reach for the suicidal person. Family members and friends can play a crucial role in the recovery of the suicidal individual by picking up cues that their loved one is distressed. As stated, clues that can indicate that someone may be depressed or suicidal can include changes in the distressed person's behavior, such as sleeping or eating more or less than usual. Other clues might be a change in weight, appearance, or mood; hearing direct or indirect statements about wishing to be dead; or seeing evidence of the distressed person giving away belongings or having a preoccupation with death. Some suicidal individuals may not be able to ask for help for a multitude of reasons. They may fear that they will not be understood or believed, they may fear that they will be "put away," or they may be so depressed that they cannot communicate what they are experiencing to another person. Family members, friends, and co-workers are often the first people to observe signs that someone they are close to is in trouble. A concerned other can then follow up by asking the distressed person questions, listening to her, taking her seriously, and facilitating a referral to a professional. If there is ever any question that the distressed individual is in imminent danger of self-harm, it is imperative that concerned others call 911 immediately.

If the suicidal individual is able to reach out and ask for help, it is vital that the person receiving the information take it seriously. Help may be requested of family members and friends in an indirect and ambiguous fashion, such as the individual stating that he "doesn't have much to live for anymore" or "it would be better if I weren't around." The untrained family member or friend may not understand that this could be an opening to begin a conversation with the distressed person about getting help. Additionally, the untrained person may hope that this is a fleeting feeling for the loved one and fear that talking about it openly will increase the feelings of suicide. Important others need to know that talking about suicide cannot cause suicide; in fact, talking about suicide can sometimes begin the process of recovery. When the suicidal person knows that he is being taken seriously and feels understood, he may be willing to take the next step and see a professional.

Unfortunately, as hard as it may be for the suicidal person to ask for assistance, she may have to do so more than once and in a more direct fashion. If she is not taken seriously or is minimized in her first request for help, the suicidal person may need to seek assistance from more than one person. Requesting help can require a Herculean effort from the depressed person, who may be experiencing lethargy and have diminished energy. It is important for the distressed individual to remember, however, that it only takes one person to listen and understand to help decrease her isolation and begin the process of getting help. The suicidal person needs to keep talking until someone listens and takes seriously what she is saying. Family members and friends need to trust their instincts and not hope that their loved one is in a phase that will pass. Important others need to be direct if concerned, ask questions, and offer to help with setting up appointments with a counselor. A life may be saved by the validation and support of a concerned family member or friend.

The more isolated suicidal person may not have a close-knit group of family members or friends that he can talk to or who may notice when there are dramatic changes in his behavior. This isolation can be especially dangerous and add to the suicidal individual's feelings of loneliness and depression. These people may have contact with others only at the workplace or school environment, where they may be even less likely to disclose their feelings of distress. Resources exist for these individuals in the form of direct contact with any number of community organizations, which include their local mental health clinic, the National Suicide Prevention Lifeline, and any local individual counselor. Contact can be initiated with a local mental health clinic or a private counselor through directory listings under the heading "Counselors." The direct number for the National Suicide Prevention Lifeline is 1-800-273-TALK (8255). This number will route any national call to a hotline nearest the caller and to a person who is available to listen and provide information and referrals 24 hours a day, 7 days a week. Other community resources include religious leaders, primary health care providers, support groups, and law enforcement. The same resources can be utilized by family members and friends if they have concerns about a loved one being suicidal and don't know what to do. Hotlines are staffed by individuals who are trained to know how to help both the person who is feeling thoughts of self-harm and the concerned others who may not know how to assist their loved one.

A BASIC RECOVERY PLAN FOR THE SUICIDAL PERSON

The first step in any recovery plan is to recognize that there is a problem and to be willing to get help for it. This is no different for the depressed and suicidal person. He must be willing to understand that he has a problem and reach out for assistance. Although this may sound simple, it is not. Depression, by its nature, creates difficulty with organization and action. The depressed person may not be able to think through the options that he has and then may not have the energy to follow through. If this person takes an initial step by speaking with a concerned other and then feels misunderstood, he may retreat. Gathering phone numbers to call a professional and then making the calls also takes organization and energy. There are times that some counselors may not be taking new patients or may not return calls promptly; someone who is depressed can become discouraged easily and may decide not to pursue other counseling options. While this initial step can present hurdles, it is important for the depressed person to remain on his mission and obtain help. He must keep calling until a connection is established with either a concerned other or a professional.

Once the depressed person has made the first call to a hotline or to a counselor, she has set the journey to recovery in place. Most often a connection will be established during the first visit with a counselor, and future visits will be arranged. It is important to know, however, that there are times that a first visit with a therapist does not satisfy the client. The client may not feel heard or understood, or the client and counselor may not be a good fit. This is not unusual; it is part of the process of finding the best help that can be found for that particular individual. Having a good connection with a counselor can be of great importance in healing. Meeting one or two therapists and choosing the one who is the best match can be empowering and instrumental in recovery. In the cases where the first therapist does not feel like a good fit, the client will need to try again with another counselor. She needs to keep trying until she feels she has found a counselor who can understand and help her.

Once a therapeutic relationship with a counselor has been established the counselor will conduct an assessment of the client to determine the plan for treatment.

This assessment may be formal or informal and will most likely consist of the counselor taking a history of the client and asking questions about current symptoms, behaviors, thoughts, and feelings. The therapist may suggest that the client also be evaluated for medication if she thinks this could be of benefit to the client. While some individuals will not be ready to begin medication, if the counselor recommends an evaluation, it would be a good idea to at least attend the medication assessment session. This session is scheduled with a psychiatric nurse practitioner or a psychiatrist who specializes in mental health medications. The client can think of this evaluation as an information-gathering session. She can listen to the recommendations, think about them, and, at some point, if she is ready, she will have the knowledge of how to proceed. There will also be times that medication will not be recommended.

The counselor that the individual has chosen will work with the client to decide upon a treatment plan that may include elements such as cognitive therapy, developing coping strategies, and interpersonal coaching. If the client is actively suicidal and the counselor determines that she may be at risk for self-harm, hospitalization may be recommended or required. If the client has suicidal thoughts but no plan for self-harm, the therapist will work with the client to establish a safety plan.

Each individual's recovery plan will be based on his own particular set of life circumstances and determined by clinician and client together. The therapeutic relationship between client and counselor can become a safe environment in which goals are set. These goals are then worked on until they are met and the depression and suicidal thoughts ease and diminish. The relationship that the patient has with his counselor is a unique and important one. Within the bounds of this relationship the patient can begin to design a new world that brings him greater comfort and improved functioning in the world.

COPING STRATEGIES

In the therapeutic counseling relationship coping strategies will be uniquely designed for the specific individual. These strategies will be dependent upon client history and the current thoughts and behaviors of the client. The therapist will work with the client to design strategies that fit her personality and lifestyle; it will be a joint venture into recovery. Each coping strategy will build upon the next until the client can step forth into the world ready to manage any relapse she may experience in the future with knowledge and skills.

There are universal coping techniques that can be utilized by anyone; some of these strategies will be described in the next few paragraphs. The strategies that are discussed in this chapter will include minimizing the use of alcohol or drugs, using positive self-talk, setting healthy boundaries, letting go, exercise, and surrounding oneself with people who are supportive and comforting. These are simple coping strategies and, when used in conjunction with therapy, can help to decrease depression and suicidal thoughts and can improve self-esteem.

Reducing the Use of Substances

Alcohol and drugs are sometimes used by people in distress to self-soothe. It may seem that alcohol, over-the-counter medications, or prescription drugs can relieve distress by helping with sleep, improving socialization, or blunting negative feelings. These positive responses are temporary and fleeting, and do not remove the underlying conditions that may have caused the despair in the first place. Alcohol and over-the-counter medication that is used to assist with sleep can later lead to further sleep disruption. Social impairment may occur when drugs and alcohol are utilized to help someone interact with others. Negative feelings may initially be blunted with the use of substances, but over time negative feelings can increase rather than decrease. The use of alcohol or drugs can further distort the thinking of someone who may be experiencing depression and can lead to dependence on the substance being used. The paradox is that initially substances may seem to help; however, the reality is that these substances can eventually compound all of the negative effects of the depression that is being masked. The use of alcohol or drugs, including sleeping pills for depression, should be limited unless they are prescribed by a physician.

Positive Self-Talk

Positive self-talk is a simple technique. It is a strategy that begins to change the continual negative chatter that some people repeat to themselves either consciously or unconsciously. Negative thoughts are often automatic and may have begun at a very young age. These negative thoughts can be quite ingrained in the way in which the person thinks about himself. Many negative self-expressions have originated from a critical caregiver during early childhood and then been adopted by the individual. These negative thoughts are self-defeating and perpetuate and solidify poor self-esteem and depression. Adopting positive self-talk can be a difficult coping strategy to implement for people who have a poor sense of self or who are feeling depressed. These individuals may not believe that there is anything good about them; thus, using positive language may seem untruthful to them. They can begin with a simple mantra, "I am okay just the way I am." While these people may not believe that they are "okay" in the beginning, the more they replace a negative thought with a positive thought, the more this belief will become solidified. It is important to remember that negative thoughts have been ingrained and repeated for years; the replacement of them will take time, and the belief about the positive will follow.

Changing negative self-talk requires three basic steps. The first step is to notice the negative thought; these thoughts are automatic and can be subtle. Once the thought has been identified, the individual needs to mindfully and gently push the thought aside, which is the second step. The last step is to replace the negative thought with a positive thought. This process may sound easy, but the negative thoughts have probably become entrenched after many years of repetition. They can be changed, but it requires diligence and practice. As stated, some individuals think they cannot replace the negative thought with a positive one because they do not believe the positive affirmation. For example, replacing "I am attractive" for the long-repeated negative thought "I am ugly" may feel dishonest for those who have become conditioned to truly believe they are unattractive. However, using the words, even if they are not believed at first, will eventually lead to a shift in core feelings about the self. Using positive self-talk can require a leap of faith; the process will work if it is practiced. The negative self-beliefs will change if the positive replacement thoughts continue, but this process requires time and patience.

Setting Boundaries

Setting healthy boundaries is an excellent coping skill to develop. There are some people who have never learned to say no and, therefore, spend their lives feeling overwhelmed and underappreciated. Setting a boundary for the first time can require considerable emotional energy, but it does become easier over time. The reward for setting a boundary is generally immediate. For example, when a task is refused, then the time is freed up for something else. This positive reinforcement can be powerful and help to provide incentive for setting further boundaries. Having healthy boundaries is a way to develop and preserve a strong sense of self. It is a healthy way in which one protects one's personal space and the space of others.

For individuals who need to develop boundaries, a good place to begin may be in reducing the time and effort spent with or on abusive/neglectful others. Many times people with poor self-esteem allow others who can be physically or emotionally abusive to control their lives. Setting boundaries with the time that is spent with these difficult others can be done slowly so that it does not feel overwhelming or frightening to the person setting the boundary. Begin setting a boundary by letting the telephone machine pick up messages and screen calls. Return only the calls that are received from someone that is caring and gives back emotional support. Surround oneself with caring others instead of those who are always making requests or who are belittling. Setting boundaries is another skill that takes time to develop, and the support of a counselor can be especially helpful in addressing the issues that arise as one learns this strategy.

It can also be helpful to begin to set boundaries by saying "no." Saying no can seem to be impossible to someone who has always set out to please others. However, when there is no ability to be discerning and someone is always accommodating to everyone else, resentment will build. The pleaser finds himself with little or no time for himself. He also may feel as if everyone else depends on him and that he never has people reach out to support him. What the person with no boundaries must remember is that others cannot read his mind. When someone asks for a favor and the response is affirmative, the person who has asked for the favor assumes that everything is fine. This person cannot know that the pleaser is fuming inside and does not want to provide the service that has been requested. It is up to the individual to set clear boundaries and say no if he does not want to accommodate the request. The first few times that someone takes the risk to say no can be frightening. There may be a fear that others will be angry at him or that he will be abandoned. Remarkably, when someone gathers up the courage to say "I just can't do that right now," he finds that others understand. In setting boundaries and learning to say no, it can be helpful to develop a handful of brief responses or sound bites to use when others make requests.

Examples of these sound bites include

- "I'm sorry; I'm really tied up for the next week."
- "I wish I could help, but I have too much on my own plate right now."
- "It sounds like it could be fun, but I have other plans for the weekend."
- "I prefer to spend some time alone."

Brief responses without too much explanation are heard better by others. When justifications are added or the individual feels as if she needs to provide a detailed series of reasons that she is saying no, the message can be lost. Try to stick with a short sentence and then, if the other person continues to press, use another variation of the brief response, such as, "I just can't; I have too much to do." Keep it short and sweet. A boundary has then been set.

In the aftermath of setting boundaries for the first time, the individual may experience feelings of guilt. These feelings are normal, and it is important not to react to them. Once the boundary has been set, the hardest part of the work has been completed. Notice the feelings of guilt and hold the boundary. As boundaries become more familiar and are set more frequently, the feelings of guilt will diminish.

Setting boundaries is a healthy practice and a wonderful coping skill during times of stress. While coping skills are more easily developed and practiced when life is at its best, they can be learned and utilized at any time.

Letting Go

Letting go is a coping skill that can be developed over time. To be able to let go is a learning process. Every small step that can be taken to let go of emotional baggage will make the journey of life lighter. Some individuals fear that to let go means to stop caring; this is not so. Letting go means to care deeply and understand that control of external circumstances is not possible. One cannot control what happened in the past, but one can work to let go of the anger and resentment that they may carry. The reality is that there is very little ability to hold true control over other people, situations, and outcomes. Once a person can let go of the idea that he can have control over others and their environment, the focus can be turned inward. Once the focus is turned inward, toward the self, rather than others, true change is possible. As the focus shifts from the external to the internal, it enables each person to work on himself and address his own life instead of trying to change everything else. Letting go provides freedom for a deeper love of self and others.

It is much easier to look at the external world and others and hope that they will change so that things can improve. It is much more difficult for the individual to focus on what she might do to make her life better. Letting go of expectations for others requires practice and self-talk. In addition to letting go of the expectations that are held for others, it is important to begin to let go of issues in the past that cannot be changed. To ruminate on an incident from the past or an upcoming event does not change the fact that the event occurred or change the outcome of the upcoming situation. The only purpose the rumination has is to distance oneself from the present moment and the experiences that one could be having. Letting go of ruminations, like the other coping skills discussed, requires practice. Human beings are very skilled at worrying about what has just happened, what happened 10 years ago, and what could happen next week. While there may never be complete freedom from worry about what has passed or what is to come, with practice the worry can be minimized. As with many of the other coping skills, self-talk is crucial. Once rumination or worry is noticed, the individual needs to gently remind herself that she does not need to think about the issue right now. She needs to guide herself back to the here and now. The thoughts may creep back in, and, once again, as soon as they are noticed, they must be gently pushed away. Over time the thoughts will space themselves out and the individual will find herself more often in the present moment. Rather than agonizing about what has passed, what is to come, and what others are doing, the focus turns inward. This is the only true place for change.

Other basic coping skills include correcting sleep patterns, eating correctly, exercising, self-soothing (hot baths, special tea, beach walks, music), and surrounding oneself with loving family and friends. Keeping to a routine is also an important way to maintain consistency and expectation.

Medical intervention may be necessary to assist with some of the strategies. For example, sleep disruption may be biologically based and require medication to improve the sleep cycle. Medication may also be necessary to assist with needed improvement in energy to invest in building coping skills. While some of the coping skills can be mastered without medication, the work to learn and practice the skills is much easier with medication when it is warranted.

Finding New Meaning

The depressed and suicidal person may have a worldview that has been filled with despair and hopelessness. He may have wondered if life is worth living and may have contemplated suicide. As this person begins to reach out to concerned others and can see a glimmer of hope, a small shift is created. Therapy, surrounding oneself with loving others, medication, and coping skills can all combine to create a new way of being in the world for the person who once wanted to die. Separately, each of these resources can have some impact on the depressed person; combined, they are formidable tools in the battle against depression. The prognosis for an individual with depression and suicidal thought who is treated with therapy and medication is excellent. The medication addresses the biological needs of the individual while the therapy works to build cognitive skills, coping skills, and positive interpersonal relationships. New meaning will be co-created between therapist and client, and the client will rejoin the world with a new outlook. As the individual reemerges from his depression, he will see the world through a different lens and can design his life plan in any new way he desires. He will have learned the skills and resources to deal with depression if it should return; he will have a new hope instilled in him that life can be a happier experience for him.

5

Suicide Prevention:
Warning Signs and How to Help

This chapter provides simplified information regarding the warning signs of depression and suicide and includes what helpers can do to intervene. The first "cheat sheet" provides observable signs that may indicate someone is thinking about killing themselves. The second "cheat sheet" provides a detailed list of what a person can do to help avert a suicide in another. It gives the reader words to use if they believe someone is in jeopardy of a suicide attempt, and encouragement to speak up. The information found in the cheat sheets comes from Maine Youth Suicide Prevention, the American Foundation for Suicide Prevention, and the American College Health Association.

WARNING SIGNS

Get immediate help if there are direct statements about imminent self-harm or there is the presence of a weapon. For example:

- The individual is threatening to hurt or kill him or herself; or if he or she is seeking a way to kill him or herself by trying to locate a gun, pills, or other lethal means (if this occurs, get immediate help by taking the person directly to a counselor or emergency room; if s/he

refuses, call 911 or the National Suicide Prevention Lifeline at 1-800-273-TALK [8255])
- There is the presence of a weapon (call 911 immediately)

The following warning signs are not an immediate crisis but can warrant attention and the help of a professional:

- Talking or writing about death, dying, or suicide
- Dramatic mood swings or a mood disorder
- Low self-worth
- History of previous suicide attempts
- Impulsivity
- Withdrawing from family and friends and becoming isolated
- Hopelessness
- Increased drug or alcohol use and increased high-risk behaviors such as driving recklessly or getting into fights
- Ongoing sadness and loss of interest in ordinary activities
- Irritability or rage
- Difficulty with sleeping or sleeping all the time
- Change in eating habits and weight
- Difficulty concentrating and making decisions
- Fatigue
- Anxiety, agitation
- Giving things away; discussing the hereafter, wills, funerals
- Recent major loss (a friend to suicide, a parent to death, loss of an important relationship, family divorce)
- Academic or financial stress (failing a major test, losing a job)
- Member of a higher risk group such as: adolescents, runaways and the homeless, elderly, white men (for completed suicide), women (for suicide attempts), LGBTQ persons, Native Americans, Pacific Islanders, Native Alaskans who is experiencing other signs of depression listed above

HOW TO HELP

The thought of suicide can be very frightening and confusing to someone wanting to help. This confusion may stop the helper from reaching out for fear of embarrassing one's self or the other person, or making things worse. It is important to know that talking to another about suicide will not cause them to become suicidal or attempt suicide. It may feel awkward or uncomfortable, but if you suspect that someone is considering suicide, you may be able to help them find hope and avert killing him or herself just by speaking up. The act of showing someone that you care can be meaningful to another, and can have very positive consequences. Taking action may save a life. If there is an immediate threat of suicide or a weapon, call 911. Otherwise, the following are some things you can say and do:

- Express your concern by saying "I am worried about you because . . ."
- Ask the question about suicide in a direct, caring way such as, "Are you thinking about suicide or killing yourself?"
- Do not promise to keep the person's suicidal thoughts to yourself. If he or she asks you to, you can say something like, "I'm sorry, but I am too worried about you to keep this secret." The individual may be angry at you, but you will have done the right thing by getting help.
- Let the person know that he or she is not alone, and that there is help.
- Offer to call the crisis hotline, or walk with the person to see the counselor if there is one available; or offer to call to make a counseling appointment and offer to go along.
- Offer to call a family member to come and support the person.
- Remember that you are not responsible for another's depression or suicidal intentions. You cannot fix another's life or change how another thinks or feels. Try not to give advice; instead, listen to the person and be supportive.
- If the person refuses help, you can call the National Suicide Prevention Lifeline to get suggestions and to have support for yourself (1-888-273-TALK [8255]).
- Speak to a counselor yourself if there is one available at your school or employment; or make an appointment with a counselor for yourself if the worry consumes you or if you become overwhelmed.
- Remember that it is never your fault if someone does commit suicide. It is a decision that they have made, and sometimes no amount of assistance can change the person's decision to die.

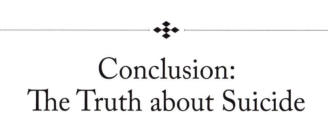

6

Conclusion:
The Truth about Suicide

Brian had been hospitalized three times for serious suicide attempts. He was considered to be in the high-risk group for completing suicide as he had many of the factors that can lead to suicide. Brian was fairly isolated with few friends or concerned family members; he was middle aged; he had periods of drinking heavily; and his family history gave evidence of generations of family members suffering from depression. His great-grandfather had killed himself with a shotgun before Brian was born. Even more worrisome, Brian felt very hopeless and really wanted to die.

During his previous hospitalizations Brian was connected with community supports and resources. He did not follow through with either the connections that were provided to him or with his medication. His depression deepened, and by the third hospitalization his therapist began to feel helpless herself in finding ways to help Brian. She decided to make changes in his treatment plan. Although the therapist had recommended Alcoholics Anonymous (AA) in the past, for the first time she connected Brian with a sponsor from AA while he was still hospitalized.

Brian had some internal resiliencies that had not yet been tapped through his therapy. His AA sponsor made an easy connection with Brian as he reminded Brian of an uncle who used to take him fishing and spend time with him when he was a child. Upon Brian's discharge from the hospital, the sponsor accompanied him to several AA meetings. Brian began to make associations with others who he felt understood him. His sponsor made it a requirement of his involvement with Brian to continue on his medication, and for the first time Brian began to experience the benefits of the antidepressants. As his depression lessened, Brian's cognitive functioning improved. He was bright, which was another of his resiliencies, and soon began to use some of the cognitive techniques he learned in his therapy to change his negative thinking. The AA meetings that he attended daily also kept him focusing on what was positive and significantly decreased his isolation. Brian described feeling like "himself" for the first time he could remember.

With the combination of medication, therapy, and AA, Brian's thoughts of death and dying diminished and over time became a distant memory. If he began to experience thoughts of suicide, Brian had the energy and desire to reach out for help to his support system. His collaborations at AA strengthened to become friendships and "family of choice."

When Brian told his story in AA, he sometimes couldn't believe he was the same person he was describing to the group. He talked about his childhood and his alcoholic, depressed father and mother who worked all the time and never had time for him. He recalled his first drink at the age of 12 and how the first years of drinking made him feel better about himself and helped him forget his loneliness. He remembered how he always isolated himself from others and then drank to console himself. Brian described how the alcohol contributed to the state of depression that he had always experienced, and how he wanted to die and end the cycle of drinking and depression that never seemed to end. Every time Brian would get into a relationship, his drinking would become a problem for his partner, who would eventually leave him, increasing his wish to die. He described his first suicide attempt by gunshot and how the police broke down his door to rescue him. He recalled not caring whether he lived or died, and being resistant to everything his counselor would suggest to help him recover. When he told his story to the group, he would shake his head with some disbelief. Now that his head was clear from the alcohol and his depression had lifted, he could clearly see the toxic cycle he had been caught in. He talked about his inability to reach out and the fact that when someone tried to help him, he rejected them.

Brian also told the group about his deep gratefulness. He looked back at the journey of his life and could see that others could easily have given up on him, but did not. He described his first glimmer of hope in life as the connection with his sponsor, who was someone he felt could understand him. His sponsor pushed him to find the resiliencies that were buried and to focus on those, not his deficits. He also knew that he had been determined to die and that if he had continued down the road he was headed that he would have eventually completed suicide. While his hospitalizations and his therapist could not dissuade him off the path to suicide, their attention bought him time until he found his path to life.

THE TRUTH ABOUT SUICIDE

The first real truth about suicide is that if someone decides that they are going to die, they will eventually find a way to kill themselves. No other single person has control over another; while there may be ways to intervene in a suicidal act, there will be other moments and opportunities to complete the suicide. If someone has decided to die by their own hand, ultimately their death may not be stopped. Important others do not have the control to stop a loved one's death if they are determined to die. If those that survive suicide can come to understand and accept this, they may begin to find their own path to recovery.

While this truth is real and profound, there are other important truths regarding suicide. There is help for the suicidal person. There are causes to suicidal feelings and behaviors that may come from early formation of the self or later life events. The good news is that for each cause of suicidal thought, there is an intervention that can alter the course of action leading to completed suicide. The key is either for the suicidal person to reach out for help or for a concerned other to help propel the individual towards assistance. Once the cause(s) of suicidal thoughts are identified, a treatment plan and resources can be put in place to make changes and improve quality of life. The evidence is that treatment of depression and suicidality is highly successful with a combination of therapy and medication. This is very good news; the task remains to propel the person who experiences suicidal tendencies to professional assistance. There are many internal and external resources that can be tapped to assist the suicidal person in their healing journey, once they are engaged in professional help. Not all individuals will be willing to begin medication or to engage in therapy. There are times that one method of treatment is enough to manage the suicidal thoughts. Building outside supports and creating a "team" of involved others to be available to the person who struggles with suicide may be enough to thwart suicidal intent in some individuals. This team of involved others does not necessarily need to be a formal one; it can include support groups such as AA or Al-Anon, family members, therapy, crisis workers, friends, spiritual groups, and cultural connections. No one should be in the position of feeling solely responsible for the well-being of someone who suffers with depression. If a concerned other finds him or herself in this position, s/he should seek professional support.

Another truth about suicide is that there is also help for those who survive the loss of a loved one to suicide. When a friend or family member completes suicide, everything changes. The world doesn't seem the same. Others do not understand the profound loss. The grief is huge and incomparable to other losses. The survivor often experiences guilt and shame and wonders if they could have somehow stopped the suicide. Survivors may experience troubling symptoms themselves, which can include depression, suicidal thoughts, trouble sleeping and eating, difficulty concentrating, uncontrollable emotions such as crying or anger, and nightmares. The survivor may also need professional intervention if the symptoms are prolonged. As with the suicidal person, the key is to reach out for help, because it is waiting and available.

In almost all cases, suicide is a very difficult event to comprehend. This book attempts to share understanding of just how the suicidal mind can develop in the young person and impact later life functioning as an adult. This book aims to offer hope to the suicidal person, and support concerned others in providing clear intervention strategies.

Reach out, to save a life.

Appendix: Resources

The resources provided here are intended for the use of those who may be feeling depressed or suicidal themselves, and for family, friends, and survivors of suicide. They are also for use by professionals who want to learn more about suicide intervention and for people in the general public who may have an interest in providing donations, research, or learning more about suicide.

1. National Suicide Prevention Lifeline: 1-800-273-TALK (8255)
Web site: http://www.suicidepreventionhotline.org/
The National Suicide Prevention Lifeline provides the public with immediate help for anyone who is feeling suicidal or is concerned about a loved one who may be suicidal. The crisis workers are on call 24 hours a day, seven days a week and will connect the caller with a crisis worker in his area so that he can talk with someone who cares and receive referrals to community supports as requested. Those who are experiencing suicidal thoughts and feelings themselves can call this number as well as those who may be concerned about a family member, co-worker, or friend. The calls are free and confidential. This is an excellent resource if you are someone who is feeling depressed or suicidal. You will be connected with a professional who can help. It is also a good resource for

concerned others who have questions about how to assist people in getting the help they need. This hotline can direct concerned others to help in dealing with their own feelings regarding a suicidal loved one or the completed suicide of a family member, friend, or colleague.

2. The Suicide Prevention Resource Center : 1-800-273-8255 (TALK)
Web site: http://www.sprc.org
The Center provides states, government agencies, private organizations, colleges and universities, and suicide survivor and mental health consumer groups with access to information and experience that supports their efforts to develop programs, implement interventions, and promote policies to prevent suicide. A feature of this site is that it provides information for each state in a drop-down menu.

3. American Foundation for Suicide Prevention: 1-888-333-AFSP
Web site: http://www.afsp.org
E-mail inquiry: inquiry@afsp.org
The American Foundation for Suicide Prevention is dedicated to understanding and preventing suicide through research and education, and reaching out to people with mood disorders and those impacted by suicide.

4. American Association for Suicidology: 1-202-237-2280
Web site: http://www.suicidology.org
The primary goal of the American Association for Suicidology is to understand and prevent suicide. This association promotes research, public awareness programs, and public education for professionals and volunteers. The association is also notable as a clearinghouse on information regarding suicide.

5. Suicide Prevention Action Network USA: 1-202-449-3600
The Suicide Prevention Action Network (SPAN) is dedicated to preventing suicide through public education and awareness, community engagement, and federal, state, and local grassroots advocacy. SPAN seeks to empower those who have been touched by suicide.

6. Stop a Suicide Today: 1-781-239-0071
Web site: http://www.stopasuicide.org
Stop a Suicide Today is a program that provides information on signs of depression and facts about suicide and mental illness. This program also provides information on how to help a friend, links to the National

Depression Screening Test, and information on finding a professional in a particular geographical area, as well as information for survivors.

7. Suicide Reference Library
Web site: http://www.suicidereferencelibrary.com
The Suicide Reference Library was created as an outreach project by volunteers and provides information for those who are involved in suicide awareness, grief support, and educational activities.

8. The Centre for Suicide Prevention: 403-254-3900
Web site: http://www.suicideinfo.ca/
The Centre for Suicide Prevention is a nonprofit organization in Calgary, Alberta, with three primary goals. The center provides information regarding suicide in a specialized library and resource center. It also provides caregiver training in suicide intervention, awareness, bereavement, crisis management, and related topics. Additionally, the center supports research on suicide and suicidal behavior.

9. Parents, Families and Friends of Lesbians and Gays (PFLAG): 202-467-8180
Web site: http://community.pflag.org
E-mail inquiry: info@pflag.org
PFLAG promotes the well-being of gay, lesbian, transgendered, and bisexual persons and represents the families and friends of lesbian, gay, bisexual, and transgendered persons. The information on this Web site may assist these individuals by providing support and connection to those who deal with depression and suicidality that may result from being a member of an underrepresented population.

10. Survivors of Suicide
Web site: http://www.survivorsofsuicide.com
Survivors of Suicide is an independently owned and operated Web site designed to help those who have lost a loved one to suicide. This Web site provides information so that all those who have lost someone to suicide can begin to resolve their grief and pain in their own personal manner.

11. National Institute of Mental Health (NAMI): 1-866-615-6464
Web site: http://nimh.nih.gov
E-mail inquiry: nimhin@nih.gov
NAMI is a national organization dedicated to research that is focused on the understanding, treatment, and prevention of mental disorders and the

promotion of mental health. Information and links to research regarding suicide statistics and prevention can be found at this Web site.

12. The Office of Minority Health (OMH): 1-240-453-2883
Web site: http://minorityhealth.hhs.gov/
E-mail inquiry: info@omhrc.gov
The Office of Minority Health provides information on health issues specific to African Americans, American Indians, Alaska Natives, Asian Americans, Hispanics, Native Hawaiians, and Pacific Islanders. This resource center collects and provides information on a variety of health topics, including substance abuse and depression. The information on this site regarding suicide is limited, however.

13. The Compassionate Friends: 630-990-0010
Web site: http://www.compassionatefriends.org
E-mail inquiry: nationaloffice@compassionatefriends.org
The Compassionate Friends is a national association designed to assist families in the positive resolution of grief following the death of a child of any age and to provide information that will help others to be supportive.

14. National Organization for People of Color against Suicide (NOPCAS): 202-549-6039
Web site: http://www.nopcas.org
E-mail inquiry: info@nopcas.com
The National Organization for People of Color against Suicide was formed to address the tragic epidemic of suicide in minority communities. This organization seeks to improve knowledge for professionals, share coping methods, educate bereaved family and friends, share information on suicide prevention and intervention, and provide insight on depression.

15. The Dougy Center: 503-775-5683
Web site: http://www.dougy.org
The Dougy Center is a national center that provides resources and support for children and teens who are grieving the death of a parent, sibling, or friend.

16. The National Center for Disease Control and Prevention (CDC): 1-800-311-3435 or 404-498-1515

Web site: http://www.cdc.gov

The CDC's mission is to promote health and quality of life by preventing and controlling disease, injury, and disability. This organization has links to many forms of information regarding depression and suicide, including suicide prevention.

References

INTRODUCTION

American Foundation for Suicide Prevention. n.d. *Surviving a Suicide Loss: A Resource and Healing Guide*. New York: American Foundation for Suicide Prevention. https://www.afsp.org/content/download/2737/50333/file/resource_healing_guide.pdf.

CHAPTER 1

Bertini, Kristine. 1995. *Marital Status and Midlife: Perceptions of Early Parenting and Perceptions of Self*. Ann Arbor: University of Michigan Press.

Bowlby, John. 1973. *Attachment and Loss*. New York: Basic Books.

Briere, John, and Marsha Runtz. 1990. "Differential Adult Symptomatology Associated with Three Types of Child Abuse Histories." *Child Abuse and Neglect* 14: 57–64.

Freud, Sigmund. 1905. *Three Essays on the Theory of Sexuality*. London: Imago.

Joiner, Thomas. 2005. *Why People Die by Suicide*. Cambridge, MA: Harvard University Press.

Jung, Carl. 1964. *Man and His Symbols*. New York: Dell.

Marshall, Mac. 1977. *Weekend Warriors: Alcohol in a Micronesian Culture*. Palo Alto, CA: Mayfield Publishing.

Mittendorfer-Rutz, Ellenor, et al. 2004. "Nurture Versus Nature: Evidence of Intrauterine Effects on Suicidal Behavior." *Lancet* 364: 1103.

Richards, Barbara M. 1999. "Suicide and Internalized Relationships: A Study from the Perspective of Psychotherapists Working with Suicidal Patients." *British Journal of Guidance and Counseling* 27(1): 85–98.

Tennant, Christopher. 1988. "Parental Loss in Childhood: Its Effect in Adult Life." *Archives of General Psychiatry* 45: 1045–50.

Twomey, Heather B., et al. 2000. "Childhood Maltreatment, Object Relations and Suicidal Behavior in Women." *Psychoanalytic Psychology* 17(2): 313–35.

Winnicott, Donald. 1963. *Maturational Processes*. New York: Basic Books.

CHAPTER 2

Satow, Roberta. 2000. *Gender and Social Life*. Allyn & Bacon.

Shneidman, Edwin. 1996. *The Suicidal Mind*. New York: Oxford University Press.

US Preventive Services Task Force. 1996. *Guide to Clinical Preventive Services*. 2nd ed. Baltimore, MD: Williams and Wilkins.

Vaknin, Samuel. 2007. *Malignant Self-Love*. Skopje, Czech Republic: Narcissus Press.

Violence Policy Center. 2002. "American Roulette: The Untold Story of Murder-Suicide in the United States." Washington, DC: Violence Policy Center.

CHAPTER 3

Bandura, Albert. 1997. *Self-Efficacy: The Exercise of Control*. New York: Freeman.

Baruth, Katey, and Jane Carroll. 2002. "A Formal Assessment of Resilience: The Baruth Protective Factors Inventory." *Journal of Individual Psychology* 58, no. 3 (Fall).

Bonanno, George. 2004. "Loss, Trauma and Human Resilience: Have We Underestimated the Human Capacity to Thrive under Extremely Adverse Events?" *American Psychologist* 59: 20–28.

Bowman, Phillip. 2006. "Role Strain and Adaptive Issues." *Counseling Psychologist* 34: 118.

Dumont, Michelle, and Marc Provost. 1999. "Resilience in Adolescents." *Journal of Youth and Adolescence* 28(3): 343–63.

Grauerholz, Liz. 2000. "An Ecological Approach to Understanding Sexual Revictimization: Linking Personal, Interpersonal, and Sociocultural Factors and Processes." *Child Maltreatment* 5: 5–17.

Papalia, Diane. 1998. *Human Development.* 7th ed. Boston: McGraw Hill.

Papalia, Diane, Sally Wendos Olds, and Ruth Feldman. 1998. *Human Development.* 7th ed. Boston: McGraw Hill.

Reivich, Karen, and Andrew Shatte. 2002. *The Resilience Factor.* New York: Random House-Doubleday.

Schumm, Jeremiah, Melissa Phillips, and Stevan Hobfoll. 2006. "Cumulative Interpersonal Trauma and Social Support as Risk and Resiliency Factors in Predicting PTSD and Depression among Inner City Women." *Journal of Traumatic Stress* 19 (Fall): 825–36.

Shaw, Jon A. 2006. "Les Enfants de Duplessis: Perspectives on Trauma and Resiliency." *Psychiatry* 69, no. 4 (Winter).

CHAPTER 4

Chemtob, Claude, et al. 1988. "Patient's Suicides: Frequency and Impact on Psychiatrists." *American Journal of Psychiatry* 145: 224–28.

Cutter, Fred. 2005. "Suggestions for Psychological Autopsy." *Suicide Prevention Triangle.*

DeAngelis, Tori. 2001. "Surviving a Patient's Suicide." *APA Monitor* 32, no. 10 (November): 70–72

Hendin, Herbert, et al. 2004. "Factors Contributing to Therapist's Distress after the Suicide of a Patient." *American Journal of Psychiatry* 161: 1442–46.

Jamison, Kay, and R. J. Baldessarini. 1999. "Effects of Medical Interventions on Suicidal Behaviors." *Journal of Clinical Psychiatry* 60: 4–6.

Jung, Carl. 1969. *Man and His Symbols.* New York: Doubleday.

Ness, David, and Cynthia Pfeffer. 1990. "Sequelae of Bereavement Resulting from Suicide." *American Journal of Psychiatry* 147(3): 279–85.

Plankun, Eric. 2005. "Responding to Clinicians after Loss of a Patient to Suicide." *Psychiatric News* 21: 10.

Sacks, Michael, et al. 1978. "Resident Response to Patient Suicide." *Journal of Psychiatric Education* 11(4): 217–26.

Shneidman, Edwin. 1971. "The Management of the Presuicidal, Suicidal and Post Suicidal Patient." *Annals of Internal Medicine*, ed. J. Hewitt Ross et al., 75: 441–58.

Steingart, Irving. 1995. *A Thing Apart.* New York: Jason Aronson.

"Suicide Prevention and Psychological Autopsy." 1988. Department of the Army (Pamphlet 600–24).

Summers, Richard, and Jacques Barber. 2003. "Therapeutic Alliance as a Measurable Psychotherapy Skill." *Academic Psychiatry* 27: 160–65.

Zaroff, Larry. 2007. "Cool Heads and Cold Heart." *New York Times*, February.

CHAPTER 5

American College Health Association. 1996. *Dealing with Depression: What Everyone Should Know.* Hanover, MD: American College Health Association.

Maine Center for Disease Control. 2011. *Suicide Prevention, It's Up to All of Us.* Augusta: Maine Department of Health and Human Services.

Index

About the Author

Kristine Bertini, PsyD, is a licensed clinical psychologist at the University of Southern Maine and in private practice. Her published works include *Understanding and Preventing Suicide: The Development of Self-Destructive Patterns and Ways to Alter Them* and *Strength for the Sandwich Generation: Help to Thrive While Simultaneously Caring for Our Kids and Our Aging Parents.* Bertini has been chair of the University Task Force on Suicide Intervention and a member of the Governor's Steering Committee on Suicide Prevention.